The Corrosion of Character

Further praise for *The Corrosion of Character*:

"Provocative . . . illuminating." —*New York Times*

"[A]n incredibly insightful book. Sennett's thought-provoking arguments will resonate in many different quarters. They will also stimulate an important national dialogue on the disorienting social and personal effects of the new 'flexible' capitalism." —William Julius Wilson, Harvard University

"Richard Sennett shows what happens to people in an economy that systematically destroys what has given meaning to human life. This beautiful and moving book by one of our finest sociologists describes, explains, and warns Europe against following the road already taken by the U.S. and, perhaps not quite so irreversibly, by Britain." —Eric Hobsbawm

"Fascinating. . . . If Sennett proves right, we are approaching changes that may affect human ways of living and self-perception as deeply as the passage from an agrarian to an industrial society." —*Die Zeit* (Germany)

"In a succinct essay of rare elegance, Richard Sennett . . . combines the forensic skills of an academic who has a sense of history with those of the social observer of the contemporary scene. The result is a tantalisingly anecdotal, often brilliant portrait of the flexible American workplace in the age of corporate re-engineering, information technology, and cult of short-termism." —Robert Taylor, *Financial Times*

"Sennett's eloquent and penetrating new book is about the shift to unstable and flexible employment. . . . He asks us to weigh the results of leanness and meanness."
—Robert M. Solow, Massachusetts Institute of Technology

"Challenges the reader to decide whether the flexibility of modern capitalism . . . is merely a fresh form of oppression."
—*Publishers Weekly* (starred review)

"A profoundly affecting argument as to what we are doing to ourselves as we reshape our work."   —*Business Week*

"Sennett argues, convincingly, that the steadily increasing insecurity experienced by workers is making it impossible for them to achieve a moral identity. . . . *The Corrosion of Character* is a remarkable synthesis of acute empirical observation and serious moral reflection."   —Richard Rorty

"Engages the heart as well as the mind. . . . Sennett makes an elegiac case for the kind of character bred in the society we are losing—one in which the dignity of ordinary, long-term, secure labour encouraged habits of dependability and long-term care for family and children." —John Lloyd, *New Statesman*

"A compassionate inspection of the times and an essential read for people concerned with business and culture."
—*Christian Science Monitor*

"One of the rare, rich books that compels you to think, that sets off genuine intellectual repercussions."
—*Atlanta Journal-Constitution*

"As compelling as fiction, keenly observant and written with grace and passion, *The Corrosion of Character* is megatrends plus morality. . . . Urgent reading for anyone who would understand the world today. Though we are all connoisseurs of chaos now, we need, more than we know, Sennett's voice of passionate reason."   —*Providence Sunday Journal*

"Sennett's *The Corrosion of Character* is substantial and serious, and many will find disturbing his assessment of the personal cost of flexible employment."
—Anthony Elliott, *The Age*

THE
Corrosion of Character

The Personal Consequences of Work
in the New Capitalism

RICHARD SENNETT

W. W. Norton & Company
New York   London

In Memory of Isaiah Berlin

For information about permission to reproduce selections from this book, write to Permissions, W. W. Norton & Company, Inc., 500 Fifth Avenue, New York, NY 10110.

The text and display of this book are composed in ITC Century Light
Desktop composition by Roberta Flechner
Manufacturing by Quebecor Printing, Fairfield Inc.
Book design by Charlotte Staub

Library of Congress Cataloging-in-Publication Data

Sennett, Richard, 1943–
The corrosion of character : the personal consequences of work in the new capitalism / Richard Sennett.
p. cm.
Includes bibliographical references and index.
ISBN 0-393-04678-8
1. Working class—United States. 2. Work ethic—United States.
3. Labor—United States. I. Title
HD8072.5.S46   1998
305.5'62—dc21   98-17106
CIP
ISBN 0-393-31987-3 pbk.

W. W. Norton & Company, Inc.
500 Fifth Avenue, New York, N.Y. 10110
www.wwnorton.com

W. W. Norton & Company Ltd.
Castle House, 75/76 Wells Street, London W1T 3QT

7 8 9 0

Contents

Preface 9

1. DRIFT 15
*How personal character is attacked
by the new capitalism*

2. ROUTINE 32
An evil of the old capitalism

3. FLEXIBLE 46
The restructuring of time

4. ILLEGIBLE 64
*Why modern forms of labor are
difficult to understand*

5. RISK 76
*Why risk-taking has become disorienting
and depressing*

6. THE WORK ETHIC 98
How the work ethic has changed

7. FAILURE 118
Coping with failure

8. THE DANGEROUS
PRONOUN 136
*Community as a remedy
for the ills of work*

Appendix: Statistical Tables 149

Notes 159

Index 167

Preface

Today the phrase "flexible capitalism" describes a system which is more than a permutation on an old theme. The emphasis is on flexibility. Rigid forms of bureaucracy are under attack, as are the evils of blind routine. Workers are asked to behave nimbly, to be open to change on short notice, to take risks continually, to become ever less dependent on regulations and formal procedures.

This emphasis on flexibility is changing the very meaning of work, and so the words we use for it. "Career," for instance, in its English origins meant a road for carriages, and as eventually applied to labor meant a lifelong channel for one's economic pursuits. Flexible capitalism has blocked the straight roadway of career, diverting employees suddenly from one kind of work into another. The word "job" in English of the fourteenth century meant a lump or piece of something which could be carted around. Flexibility today brings back this arcane sense of the job, as people do lumps of labor, pieces of work, over the course of a lifetime.

It is quite natural that flexibility should arouse anxiety: people do not know what risks will pay off, what paths to pursue. To take the curse off the phrase "capitalist system" there developed in the past many circumlocutions, such as the "free enterprise" or "private enterprise" system. Flexibility is used today as another way to lift the curse of oppression from capitalism. In attacking rigid bureaucracy and emphasizing risk, it is claimed, flexibility gives people more freedom to shape their lives. In fact, the new order substitutes new controls rather than simply abolishing the rules of the past—but these new controls are also hard to understand. The new capitalism is an often illegible regime of power.

Perhaps the most confusing aspect of flexibility is its impact on personal character. The old English speakers, and indeed writers going back to antiquity, were in no doubt about the meaning of "character": it is the ethical value we place on our own desires and on our relations to others. Horace writes that the character of a man depends on his connections to the world. In this sense, "character" is a more encompassing term than its more modern offspring "personality," which concerns desires and sentiments which may fester within, witnessed by no one else.

Character particularly focuses upon the long-term aspect of our emotional experience. Character is expressed by loyalty and mutual commitment, or through the pursuit of long-term goals, or by the practice of delayed gratification for the sake of a future end. Out of the confusion of sentiments in which we all dwell at any particular moment, we seek to save and sustain some; these sustainable sentiments will serve our characters. Character concerns the personal traits which we value in ourselves and for which we seek to be valued by others.

How do we decide what is of lasting value in ourselves in a society which is impatient, which focuses on the immediate moment? How can long-term goals be pursued in an economy devoted to the short term? How can mutual loyalties and commitments be sustained in institutions which are constantly breaking apart or continually being redesigned? These are the questions about character posed by the new, flexible capitalism.

A QUARTER CENTURY AGO, Jonathan Cobb and I wrote a book about working-class Americans, *The Hidden Injuries of Class.* In *The Corrosion of Character,* I've taken up some of the same issues about work and character in an economy which has changed radically. *The Corrosion of Character* is intended to be a long essay rather than a short book; that is, I've tried to write out a single argument, whose sections are divided into very short chapters. In *The Hidden Injuries of Class*, Jonathan Cobb and I relied exclusively on formal interviews. Here, as befits an essay-argument, I've used more mixed and informal sources, including economic data, historical accounts, and social theories; I've also explored the daily life around me, much as an anthropologist might.

At the outset, I should point out two things about this text. The reader will often find philosophical ideas applied to or tested by the concrete experience of individuals. For this I make no apology; an idea has to bear the weight of concrete experience or else it becomes a mere abstraction. Second, I've disguised individual identities rather more heavily than one would when reporting formal interviews; this has meant changing places and times and occasionally compounding several voices into one or splitting one voice into many. These disguises put demands on the reader's trust, but not the trust a novelist would seek to earn through a well-made narrative, for that coherence is now lacking in real lives. My hope is that I have accurately reflected the sense of what I've heard, if not precisely its circumstances.

All the notes for essay text appear at the end of the text. I've also placed at the end some statistical tables, prepared by Arturo Sanchez and myself, which help illustrate some recent economic trends.

I LEARNED A GREAT DEAL about work from Jonathan Cobb a quarter century ago. I returned to this subject at the urging of Garrick Utley, and was helped in pursuing it by Bennett Harrison, Christopher Jencks, and Saskia Sassen; *The Corrosion of Character* tries to fathom some personal implications of the discoveries they all have made about the modern economy. To my graduate assistant Michael Laskawy, I owe a debt of intellectual companionship and also of forbearance in dealing with the various practical issues which attend research and writing.

This essay began as a Darwin Lecture, given at Cambridge University in 1996. The Center for Advanced Study in the Behavioral Sciences afforded me the time to write this book.

Finally, I would like to thank Donald Lamm and Alane Mason, of W. W. Norton & Company, and Arnulf Conradi and Elizabeth Ruge of Berlin Verlag, who helped me shape the manuscript.

The Corrosion of Character

ONE
Drift

Recently I met someone in an airport whom I hadn't seen
for fifteen years. I had interviewed the father of Rico (as I shall
call him) a quarter century ago when I wrote a book about
blue-collar workers in America, *The Hidden Injuries of
Class.* Enrico, his father, then worked as a janitor, and had
high hopes for this boy, who was just entering adolescence, a
bright kid good at sports. When I lost touch with his father a
decade later, Rico had just finished college. In the airline
lounge, Rico looked as if he had fulfilled his father's dreams.
He carried a computer in a smart leather case, dressed in a
suit I couldn't afford, and sported a signet ring with a crest.

Enrico had spent twenty years by the time we first met
cleaning toilets and mopping floors in a downtown office building. He did so without complaining, but also without any hype
about living out the American Dream. His work had one single
and durable purpose, the service of his family. It had taken him
fifteen years to save the money for a house, which he pur-
chased in a suburb near Boston, cutting ties with his old Italian
neighborhood because a house in the suburbs was better for
the kids. Then his wife, Flavia, had gone to work, as a presser
in a dry-cleaning plant; by the time I met Enrico in 1970, both
parents were saving for the college education of their two
sons.

What had most struck me about Enrico and his generation
was how linear time was in their lives: year after year of work-

ing in jobs which seldom varied from day to day. And along
that line of time, achievement was cumulative: Enrico and
Flavia checked the increase in their savings every week, measured their domesticity by the various improvements and ad-
ditions they had made to their ranch house. Finally, the time
they lived was predictable. The upheavals of the Great
Depression and World War II had faded, unions protected their
jobs; though he was only forty when I first met him, Enrico
knew precisely when he would retire and how much money he
would have.

Time is the only resource freely available to those at the
bottom of society. To make time accumulate, Enrico needed
what the sociologist Max Weber called an "iron cage," a bureaucratic structure which rationalized the use of time; in
Enrico's case, the seniority rules of his union about pay and
the regulations organizing his government pension provided
this scaffolding. When he added to these resources his own
self-discipline, the result was more than economic.

He carved out a clear story for himself in which his experience accumulated materially and psychically; his life thus
made sense to him as a linear narrative. Though a snob might
dismiss Enrico as boring, he experienced the years as a dramatic story moving forward repair by repair, interest payment
by interest payment. The janitor felt he became the author of
his life, and though he was a man low on the social scale, this
narrative provided him a sense of self-respect.

Though clear, Enrico's life story was not simple. I was particularly struck by how Enrico straddled the worlds of his old
immigrant community and his new suburban-neutral life.
Among his suburban neighbors he lived as a quiet, self-effac-
ing citizen; when he returned to the old neighborhood, however, he received much more attention as a man who had
made good on the outside, a worthy elder who returned each
Sunday for Mass followed by lunch followed by gossipy cof-
fees. He got recognition as a distinctive human being from
those who knew him long enough to understand his story; he
got a more anonymous kind of respect from his new neighbors

by doing what everyone else did, keeping his home and garden neat, living without incident. The thick texture of Enrico's particular experience lay in the fact that he was acknowledged in both ways, depending in which community he moved: two identities from the same disciplined use of his time.

If the world were a happy and just place, those who enjoy respect would give back in equal measure the regard which has been accorded them. This was Fichte's idea in "The Foundations of National Law"; he spoke of the "reciprocal effect" of recognition. But real life does not proceed so generously.

Enrico disliked blacks, although he had labored peaceably for many years with other janitors who were black; he disliked non-Italian foreigners like the Irish, although his own father could barely speak English. He could not acknowledge kindred struggles; he had no class allies. Most of all, however, Enrico disliked middle-class people. We treated him as though he were invisible, "as a zero," he said; the janitor's resentment was complicated by his fear that because of his lack of education and his menial status, we had a sneaking right to do so. To his powers of endurance in time he contrasted the whining self-pity of blacks, the unfair intrusion of foreigners, and the unearned privileges of the bourgeoisie.

Though Enrico felt he had achieved a measure of social honor, he hardly wanted his son Rico to repeat his own life. The American dream of upward mobility for the children powerfully drove my friend. "I don't understand a word he says," Enrico boasted to me several times when Rico had come home from school and was at work on math. I heard many other parents of sons and daughters like Rico say something like "I don't understand him" in harder tones, as though the kids had abandoned them. We all violate in some way the place assigned us in the family myth, but upward mobility gives that passage a peculiar twist. Rico and other youngsters headed up the social ladder sometimes betrayed shame about their parents' working-class accents and rough manners, but more often felt suffocated by the endless strategizing over pennies and the reckoning of time in tiny steps. These favored children wanted to embark on a less constrained journey.

Now, many years later, thanks to the encounter at the airport, I had the chance to see how it had turned out for Enrico's son. In the airport lounge, I must confess, I didn't much like what I saw. Rico's expensive suit could have been just business plumage, but the crested signet ring—a mark of elite family background—seemed both a lie and a betrayal of the father. However, circumstances threw Rico and me together on a long flight. He and I did not have one of those American journeys in which a stranger spills out his or her emotional guts to you, gathers more tangible baggage when the plane lands, and disappears forever. I took the seat next to Rico without being asked, and for the first hour of a long flight from New York to Vienna had to pry information out of him.

RICO, I LEARNED, has fulfilled his father's desire for upward mobility, but has indeed rejected the way of his father. Rico scorns "time-servers" and others wrapped in the armor of bureaucracy; instead he believes in being open to change and in taking risks. And he has prospered; whereas Enrico had an income in the bottom quarter of the wage scale, Rico's has shot up to the top 5 percent. Yet this is not an entirely happy story for Rico.

After graduating from a local university in electrical engineering, Rico went to a business school in New York. There he married a fellow student, a young Protestant woman from a better family. School prepared the young couple to move and change jobs frequently, and they've done so. Since graduation, in fourteen years at work Rico has moved four times.

Rico began as a technology adviser to a venture capital firm on the West Coast, in the early, heady days of the developing computer industry in Silicon Valley; he then moved to Chicago, where he also did well. But the next move was for the sake of his wife's career. If Rico were an ambition-driven character out of the pages of Balzac, he would never have done it, for he gained no larger salary, and he left hotbeds of high-tech activity for a more retired, if leafy, office park in Missouri. Enrico felt somewhat ashamed when Flavia went to work; Rico sees Jeannette, his wife, as an equal working partner, and has adapted to her. It was at this point, when Jeannette's career took off, that their children began arriving.

In the Missouri office park, the uncertainties of the new economy caught up with the young man. While Jeannette was promoted, Rico was downsized—his firm was absorbed by another, larger firm that had its own analysts. So the couple made a fourth move, back East to a suburb outside New York. Jeannette now manages a big team of accountants, and he has started a small consulting firm.

Prosperous as they are, the very acme of an adaptable, mutually supportive couple, both husband and wife often fear they are on the edge of losing control over their lives. This fear is built into their work histories.

In Rico's case, the fear of lacking control is straightforward: it concerns managing time. When Rico told his peers he was going to start his own consulting firm, most approved; consulting seems the road to independence. But in getting started he found himself plunged into many menial tasks, like doing his own photocopying, which before he'd taken for granted. He found himself plunged into the sheer flux of networking; every call had to be answered, the slightest acquaintance pursued. To find work, he has fallen subservient to the schedules of people who are in no way obliged to respond to him. Like other consultants, he wants to work in accordance with contracts setting out just what the consultant will do. But these contracts, he says, are largely fictions. A consultant usually has to tack one way and another in response to the changing whims or thoughts of those who pay; Rico has no fixed role that allows him to say to others, "This is what I do, this is what I am responsible for."

Jeannette's lack of control is more subtle. The small group of accountants she now manages is divided among people who work at home, people usually in the office, and a phalanx of low-level back-office clerks a thousand miles away connected to her by computer cable. In her present corporation, strict rules and surveillance of phones and e-mail disciplines the conduct of the accountants who work from home; to organize the work of the back-office clerks a thousand miles away, she can't make hands-on, face-to-face judgments, but instead must work by formal written guidelines. She hasn't experienced less bureaucracy in this seemingly flexible work arrangement; indeed, her own decisions count for less than in the days when she supervised workers who were grouped together, all the time, in the same office.

As I say, at first I was not prepared to shed many tears for this American Dream couple. Yet as dinner was served to Rico and me on our flight, and he began to talk more personally, my sympathies increased. His fear of losing control, it developed, went much deeper than worry about losing power in his job. He feared that the actions he needs to take and the way he has to live in order to survive in the modern economy have set his emotional, inner life adrift.

Rico told me that he and Jeannette have made friends mostly with the people they see at work, and have lost many of these friendships during the moves of the last twelve years, "though we stay 'netted.'" Rico looks to electronic communications for the sense of community which Enrico most enjoyed when he attended meetings of the janitors' union, but the son finds communications on-line short and hurried. "It's like with your kids—when you're not there, all you get is news later."

In each of his four moves, Rico's new neighbors have treated his advent as an arrival which closes past chapters of his life; they ask him about Silicon Valley or the Missouri office park, but, Rico says, "they don't *see* other places"; their imaginations are not engaged. This is a very American fear. The classic American suburb was a bedroom community; in the last generation a different kind of suburb has arisen, more economically independent of the urban core, but not really town or village either; a place springs into life with the wave of a developer's wand, flourishes, and begins to decay all within a generation. Such communities are not empty of sociability or neighborliness, but no one in them becomes a long-term witness to another person's life.

The fugitive quality of friendship and local community form the background to the most important of Rico's inner worries, his family. Like Enrico, Rico views work as his service to the family; unlike Enrico, Rico finds that the demands of the job interfere with achieving the end. At first I thought he was talking about the all too familiar conflict between work time and time for family. "We get home at seven, do dinner, try to find an hour for the kids' homework, and then deal with our own paperwork." When things get tough for months at a time in his consulting firm, "it's like I don't know who my kids are." He worries about the frequent anarchy into which his family plunges, and about neglecting his children, whose needs can't be programmed to fit into the demands of his job.

Hearing this, I tried to reassure him; my wife, stepson, and I had endured and survived well a similarly high-pressure life. "You aren't being fair to yourself," I said. "The fact you care so much means you are doing the best for your family you can." Though he warmed to this, I had misunderstood.

As a boy, I already knew, Rico had chafed under Enrico's authority; he had told me then he felt smothered by the small-minded rules which governed the janitor's life. Now that he is a father himself, the fear of a lack of ethical discipline haunts him, particularly the fear that his children will become "mall rats," hanging out aimlessly in the parking lots of shopping centers in the afternoons while the parents remain out of touch at their offices.

He therefore wants to set for his son and daughters an example of resolution and purpose, "but you can't just tell kids to be like that"; he has to set an example. The objective example he could set, his upward mobility, is something they take for granted, a history that belongs to a past not their own, a story which is over. But his deepest worry is that he cannot offer the substance of his work life as an example to his children of how they should conduct themselves ethically. The qualities of good work are not the qualities of good character.

As I CAME LATER TO UNDERSTAND, the gravity of this fear comes from a gap separating Enrico and Rico's generations. Business leaders and journalists emphasize the global marketplace and the use of new technologies as the hallmarks of the capitalism of our time. This is true enough, but misses another dimension of change: new ways of organizing time, particularly working time.

The most tangible sign of that change might be the motto "No long term." In work, the traditional career progressing step by step through the corridors of one or two institutions is withering; so is the deployment of a single set of skills through the course of a working life. Today, a young American with at least two years of college can expect to change jobs at least eleven times in the course of working, and change his or her skill base at least three times during those forty years of labor.

An executive for ATT points out that the motto "No long term" is altering the very meaning of work:

> In ATT we have to promote the whole concept of the work force being contingent, though most of the contingent workers are inside our walls. "Jobs" are being replaced by "projects" and "fields of work."[1]

Corporations have also farmed out many of the tasks they once did permanently in-house to small firms and to individuals employed on short-term contracts. The fastest-growing sector of the American labor force, for instance, is people who work for temporary job agencies.[2]

"People are hungry for [change]," the management guru James Champy argues, because "the market may be 'consumer-driven' as never before in history."[3] The market, in this view, is too dynamic to permit doing things the same way year after year, or doing the same thing. The economist Bennett Harrison believes the source of this hunger for change is "impatient capital," the desire for rapid return; for instance, the average length of time stocks have been held on British and

American exchanges has dropped 60 percent in the last fifteen years. The market believes rapid market return is best generated by rapid institutional change.

The "long-term" order at which the new regime takes aim, it should be said, was itself short-lived—the decades spanning the mid-twentieth century. Nineteenth-century capitalism lurched from disaster to disaster in the stock markets and in irrational corporate investment; the wild swings of the business cycle provided people little security. In Enrico's generation after World War II, this disorder was brought somewhat under control in most advanced economies; strong unions, guarantees of the welfare state, and large-scale corporations combined to produce an era of relative stability. This span of thirty or so years defines the "stable past" now challenged by a new regime.

A change in modern institutional structure has accompanied short-term, contract, or episodic labor. Corporations have sought to remove layers of bureaucracy, to become flatter and more flexible organizations. In place of organizations as pyramids, management wants now to think of organizations as networks. "Networklike arrangements are lighter on their feet" than pyramidal hierarchies, the sociologist Walter Powell declares; "they are more readily decomposable or redefinable than the fixed assets of hierarchies."[4] This means that promotions and dismissals tend not to be based on clear, fixed rules, nor are work tasks crisply defined; the network is constantly redefining its structure.

An IBM executive once told Powell that the flexible corporation "must become an archipelago of related activities."[5] The archipelago is an apt image for communications in a network, communication occurring like travel between islands—but at the speed of light, thanks to modern technologies. The computer has been the key to replacing the slow and clogged communications which occur in traditional chains of command. The fastest-growing sector of the labor force deals in computer and data-processing services, the area in which Jeanette and Rico work; the computer is now used in virtually all jobs, in many ways, by people of all ranks. (Please see Tables 1 and 7 in the Appendix for a statistical portrait.)

For all these reasons, Enrico's experience of long-term, narrative time in fixed channels has become dysfunctional. What Rico sought to explain to me—and perhaps to himself—is that the material changes embodied in the motto "No long term" have become dysfunctional for him too, but as guides to personal character, particularly in relation to his family life.

Take the matter of commitment and loyalty. "No long term" is a principle which corrodes trust, loyalty, and mutual commitment. Trust can, of course, be a purely formal matter, as when people agree to a business deal or rely on another to observe the rules in a game. But usually deeper experiences of trust are more informal, as when people learn on whom they can rely when given a difficult or impossible task. Such social bonds take time to develop, slowly rooting into the cracks and crevices of institutions.

The short time frame of modern institutions limits the ripening of informal trust. A particularly egregious violation of mutual commitment often occurs when new enterprises are first sold. In firms starting up, long hours and intense effort are demanded of everyone; when the firms go public—that is, initially offer publicly traded shares—the founders are apt to sell out and cash in, leaving lower-level employees behind. If an organization whether new or old operates as a flexible, loose network structure rather than by rigid command from the top, the network can also weaken social bonds. The sociologist Mark Granovetter says that modern institutional networks are marked by "the strength of weak ties," by which he partly means that fleeting forms of association are more useful to people than long-term connections, and partly that strong social ties like loyalty have ceased to be compelling.[6] These weak ties are embodied in teamwork, in which the team moves from task to task and the personnel of the team changes in the process.

Strong ties depend, by contrast, on long association. And more personally they depend on a willingness to make commitments to others. Given the typically short, weak ties in institutions today, John Kotter, a Harvard Business School professor, counsels the young to work "on the outside rather than on the inside" of organizations. He advocates consulting rather than becoming "entangled" in long-term employment; institutional loyalty is a trap in an economy where "business concepts, product designs, competitor intelligence, capital equipment, and all kinds of knowledge have shorter credible life spans."[7] A consultant who managed a recent IBM job shrinkage declares that once employees "understand [they can't depend on the corporation] they're marketable."[8] Detachment and superficial cooperativeness are better armor for dealing with current realities than behavior based on values of loyalty and service.

It is the time dimension of the new capitalism, rather than high-tech data transmission, global stock markets, or free trade, which most directly affects people's emotional lives outside the workplace. Transposed to the family realm, "No long term" means keep moving, don't commit yourself, and don't sacrifice. Rico suddenly erupted on the plane, "You can't imagine how stupid I feel when I talk to my kids about commitment. It's an abstract virtue to them; they don't see it anywhere." Over dinner I simply didn't understand the outburst, which seemed apropos of nothing. But his meaning is now clearer to me as a reflection upon himself. He means the children don't see commitment practiced in the lives of their parents or their parents' generation.

Similarly, Rico hates the emphasis on teamwork and open discussion which marks an enlightened, flexible workplace once those values are transposed to the intimate realm. Practiced at home, teamwork is destructive, marking an absence of authority and of firm guidance in raising children. He and Jeannette, he says, have seen too many parents who have talked every family issue to death for fear of saying "No!," parents who listen too well, who understand beautifully rather than lay down the law; they have seen as a result too many disoriented kids.

"Things have to hold together," Rico declared to me. Again, I didn't at first quite get this, and he explained what he meant in terms of watching television. Perhaps unusually, Rico and Jeannette make it a practice to discuss with their two sons the relation between movies or sitcoms the boys watch on the tube and events in the newspapers. "Otherwise it's just a jumble of images." But mostly the connections concern the violence and sexuality the children see on television. Enrico constantly spoke in little parables to drive home questions of character; these parables he derived from his work as a janitor—such as "You can ignore dirt but it won't go away." When I first knew Rico as an adolescent, he reacted with a certain shame to these homely snippets of wisdom. So now I asked Rico if he too made parables or even just drew ethical rules from his experience at work. He first ducked answering directly—"There's not much on TV about that sort of thing"—then replied, "And well, no, I don't talk that way."

Behavior which earns success or even just survival at work thus gives Rico little to offer in the way of a parental role model. In fact, for this modern couple, the problem is just the reverse: how can they protect family relations from succumbing to the short-term behavior, the meeting mind-set, and above all the weakness of loyalty and commitment which mark the modern workplace? In place of the chameleon values of the new economy, the family—as Rico sees it—should emphasize instead formal obligation, trustworthiness, commitment, and purpose. These are all long-term virtues.

This conflict between family and work poses some questions about adult experience itself. How can long-term purposes be pursued in a short-term society? How can durable social relations be sustained? How can a human being develop a narrative of identity and life history in a society composed of episodes and fragments? The conditions of the new economy feed instead on experience which drifts in time, from place to place, from job to job. If I could state Rico's dilemma more largely, short-term capitalism threatens to corrode his character, particularly those qualities of character which bind human beings to one another and furnishes each with a sense of sustainable self.

BY THE END OF DINNER, both of us were wrapped in our own thoughts. I had imagined a quarter century ago that late capitalism had achieved something like a final consummation; whether there was more market freedom, less government control, still the "system" entered into people's everyday experience as it always had, through success and failure, domination and submission, alienation and consumption. Questions of culture and character fell for me into these familiar categories. But no young person's experience today could be captured by these old habits of thought.

Rico's talk about his family had also set him, evidently, to thinking about his ethical values. When we retired to the back of the cabin to smoke, he remarked to me that he used to be a liberal, in the generous American sense of caring about the poor and behaving well to minorities like blacks and homosexuals. Enrico's intolerance of blacks and foreigners shamed his son. Since going to work, though, Rico says he has become a "cultural conservative." Like most of his peers, he loathes social parasites, embodied for him in the figure of the welfare mother who spends her government checks on booze and drugs. He has also become a believer in fixed, Draconian standards of communal behavior, as opposed to those values of "liberal parenting" which parallel the open-ended meeting at work. As an example of this communal ideal Rico told me that he approves the proposal current in some conservative circles to take away the children of bad parents and put them in orphanages.

My hackles rose and we debated furiously, smoke rising above us in a cloud. We were talking past each other. (And as I look over my notes, I see Rico also a bit enjoyed provoking me.) He knows his cultural conservatism is just that—an ide-

alized symbolic community. He has no real expectation of
shutting children up in orphanages. He has certainly had little
adult experience of the conservatism which preserves the
past; for instance, other Americans have treated him each
time he has moved as though life is just beginning, the past
consigned to oblivion. The cultural conservatism to which he
subscribes forms a testament to the coherence he feels missing in his life.

And as concerns the family, his values are no simple matter
of nostalgia. Rico in fact disliked the actual experience of rigid
parental rule such as he suffered at Enrico's hands. He would
not return to the linear time which ordered Enrico and Flavia's
existence even if he could; he looked at me with a certain dis-
gust when I told him that as a college professor, I have job
tenure for life. He treats uncertainty and risk-taking as challenges at work; as a consultant he has learned to be an adept
team player.

But these forms of flexible behavior have not served Rico in
his roles as a father or as a member of a community; he wants
to sustain social relations and to offer durable guidance. It is
against the severed ties at work, willful amnesia of his neighbors, and the specter of his children as mall rats that he asserts the *idea* of lasting values. And so Rico has become
caught in a trap.

All the specific values he cited are fixed rules: a parent says
no; a community demands work; dependence is an evil. The
vagaries of circumstance are excluded from these ethical
rules—random vagaries are what, after all, Rico wants to defend against. But it's difficult to put such timeless rules into
practice.

That difficulty appears in the language Rico uses to describe his moves the last fourteen years around the country.
Though many of these moves have not been of his own desir-
ing, he seldom used the passive voice in recounting the
events. For instance, he dislikes the locution "I was downsized"; instead, when this event broke up his life in the
Missouri office park, he declared, "I faced a crisis and I had a

decision to make." About this crisis he said, "I make my own choices; I take full responsibility for moving around so much." This sounded like his father. "Taking responsibility for yourself" was the most important phrase in Enrico's lexicon. But Rico didn't see how to act on it.

I asked Rico, "When you were downsized in Missouri, why didn't you protest, why didn't you fight back?"

"Sure, I felt angry, but that doesn't do any good. There was nothing unfair about the corporation's making its operation tighter. Whatever happened, I had to deal with the consequences. Would I ask Jeannette to move, one more time, for me? It was bad for the kids as well as her. Should I ask her? Who should I write a letter to about that?"

There was no action he could take. Even so, he feels responsible for this event beyond his control; he literally takes it into himself, as his own burden. But what does "taking responsibility" mean? His children accept mobility as just the way of the world; his wife is in fact grateful that he has been willing to move for her sake. Yet the statement "I take responsibility for moving around so much" issues from Rico as a defiant challenge. By this point in our journey, I understood that the last thing I should reply to this challenge was "How could you hold yourself accountable?" It would have been a reasonable question and an insult—*you* don't really matter.

Enrico had a somewhat fatalistic, old-world sense of people being born into a particular class or condition of life and making the very best of what is possible within those constraints. Events beyond his control, like layoffs, happened to him; then he coped. As this bit of sparring I've just quoted may make clear, Rico's sense of responsibility is more absolute. What he draws attention to is his unbending willingness to be held accountable, to that quality of character, rather than to a particular course of action. Flexibility has pushed him to assert the sheer strength of will as the essence of his own ethical character.

Assuming responsibility for events beyond one's control may seem a familiar friend—guilt—but this would wrongly characterize Rico, at least as he appeared to me. He is not self-indulgently self-accusing. Nor has he lost his nerve, faced with a society which seems to him all in fragments. The rules he frames for what a person of good character should do may seem simplistic or childish, but again this would be to judge him wrongly. He is in a way a realist; it would indeed have been meaningless for him to write a letter to his employers about the havoc they had introduced into his family. So Rico focuses on his own sheer determination to resist: he will not drift. He wants to resist particularly the acid erosion of those qualities of character, like loyalty, commitment, purpose, and resolution, which are long-term in nature. He affirms timeless values which characterize who he is—for good, permanently, essentially. His will has become static; he is trapped in the sheer assertion of values.

What is missing between the polar opposites of drifting experience and static assertion is a narrative which could organize his conduct. Narratives are more than simple chronicles of events; they give shape to the forward movement of time, suggesting reasons why things happen, showing their consequences. Enrico had a narrative for his life, linear and cumulative, a narrative which made sense in a highly bureaucratic world. Rico lives in a world marked instead by short-term flexibility and flux; this world does not offer much, either economically or socially, in the way of narrative. Corporations break up or join together, jobs appear and disappear, as events lacking connections. Creative destruction, Schumpeter said, thinking about entrepreneurs, requires people at ease about not reckoning the consequences of change, or not knowing what comes next. Most people, though, are not at ease with change in this nonchalant, negligent way.

Certainly Rico doesn't want to live as a Schumpeterian man, though in the brute struggle for survival he has done well. "Change" means just drift; Rico worries that his children will drift ethically and emotionally—but as with his employers, there is nothing like a letter he can write to his children which will guide them through time. The lessons he wants to teach them are as timeless as is his own sense of determination—which means his ethical precepts apply to any and all cases. Change's confusions and anxieties have bred in him this swing to the opposite extreme; perhaps this is why he cannot hold up his own life as an illustrative tale to his children, perhaps why, in listening to him, one has no sense of his character unfolding, or his ideals evolving.

I'VE DESCRIBED THIS ENCOUNTER BECAUSE Rico's experiences with time, place, and work are not unique; neither is his emotional response. The conditions of time in the new capitalism have created a conflict between character and experience, the experience of disjointed time threatening the ability of people to form their characters into sustained narratives.

At the end of the fifteenth century, the poet Thomas Hoccleve declared in *The Regiment of Princes,* "Allas, wher ys this worldes stabylnesse?"—a lament that appears equally in Homer or in Jeremiah in the Old Testament.[9] Through most of human history, people have accepted the fact that their lives will shift suddenly due to wars, famines, or other disasters, and that they will have to improvise in order to survive. Our parents and grandparents were filled with anxiety in 1940, having endured the wreckage of the Great Depression and facing the looming prospect of a world war.

What's peculiar about uncertainty today is that it exists without any looming historical disaster; instead it is woven into the everyday practices of a vigorous capitalism. Instability is meant to be normal, Schumpeter's entrepreneur served up as an ideal Everyman. Perhaps the corroding of character is an inevitable consequence. "No long term" disorients action over the long term, loosens bonds of trust and commitment, and divorces will from behavior.

I think Rico knows he is both a successful and a confused man. The flexible behavior which has brought him success is weakening his own character in ways for which there exists no practical remedy. If he is an Everyman for our times, his universality may lie in that dilemma.

TWO

Routine

There are good reasons Rico struggles to make sense of the time he lives. Modern society is in revolt against the routine, bureaucratic time which can paralyze work or government or other institutions. Rico's problem is what to do with himself when this revolt against routine succeeds.

At the dawn of industrial capitalism, though, it was not self-evident that routine was an evil. In the middle of the eighteenth century, it seemed that repetitive labor could lead in two quite different directions, one positive and fruitful, the other destructive. The positive side of routine was depicted in Diderot's great *Encyclopedia,* published from 1751 to 1772; the negative side of regular labor-time was portrayed most dramatically in Adam Smith's *The Wealth of Nations,* published in 1776. Diderot believed routine in work could be like any other form of rote learning, a necessary teacher; Smith believed routine deadened the mind. Today, society sides with Smith. Diderot suggests what we might lose by taking his opponent's side.

THE MOST STRIKING ARTICLES in the *Encyclopedia* to Diderot's well-bred audience were those on everyday life: articles by several authors on industry, the various crafts, and farming. These accompanied a series of engravings which illustrated how to make a chair or chisel stone. Mid-eighteenth-century drawing is marked by an elegance of line, but most artists deployed that elegance to depict scenes of aristocratic leisure or landscape; the illustrators of the *Encyclopedia* put that elegance in the service of drawing hammers, paper presses, and pile drivers. The point of both images and text was to justify the inherent dignity of labor.[10]

The particular dignity of routine appears in Volume 5 of the *Encyclopedia*, in a series of plates showing an actual paper factory, l'Anglée, which lay about sixty miles south of Paris near the town of Montargis. The paper mill is laid out like a chateau, with a main block connecting at two right angles to smaller wings; on the exterior we see parterres and allées around the mill, just as they might have looked on the grounds of a country aristocrat's home.

The setting of this model factory—so pretty to our eyes—in fact dramatizes a great transformation of labor beginning in Diderot's time: here home was separated from workplace. Up to the mid-eighteenth century, the household served as the physical center of the economy. In the countryside, families made most of the things they consumed; in cities like Paris or London, trades also were practiced in the family dwelling. In a baker's house, for instance, journeymen, apprentices, and the baker's biological family all "took their meals together, and food was provided for all, together, since all were expected to sleep and live in the house," as the historian Herbert Applebaum points out; "the cost of making bread . . . included the housing, feeding, and clothing of all the people who worked for the master. Money wages was a fraction of the cost."[11] The anthropologist Daniel Defert calls this an economy of the *domus*; instead of wage slavery, there reigned an inseparable combination of shelter and subordination to the will of a master.

Diderot depicts at L'Anglée a new order of work, cut free from the *domus*. The factory provided no workers' housing on the grounds; indeed, this factory was one of the first in France to recruit workers from far enough away that they had to ride to work, rather than walk on foot. It was also one of the first to pay adolescent workers wages directly, rather than paying their parents. The attractive, even elegant, appearance of the paper mill suggests that the engraver viewed this separation in a positive light.

What we are shown inside is also positive: order reigns. Paper pulping was in fact during the eighteenth century a messy and stinking operation; the rags used for paper were often stripped from corpses, then rotted in vats for two months to break down their fibers. At L'Anglée, though, the floors are spotless and no workers appear on the verge of vomiting. In the room where the fibers are beaten to a pulp by a stamping mill—the messiest of all activities—there are no human beings at all. In the room where the trickiest human division of labor occurred, the pulp scooped, then pressed into thin sheets, three craftsmen work with balletic coordination.

The secret of this industrial order lay in its precise routines. L'Anglée is a factory in which everything has its appointed place and everyone knows what to do. But for Diderot, routines of this sort did not imply the simple, endless mechanical repetition of a task. The schoolmaster who insists a pupil memorize fifty lines of a poem wants the poetry stored in the pupil's brain, recoverable at command and usable in judging other poems. In his *Paradox of Acting,* Diderot sought to explain how the actor or actress gradually plumbs the depths of a part by repeating the lines again and again. And these same virtues of repetition he expected to find in industrial labor.

Paper-making is not mindless; Diderot believed—again by analogy to the arts—that its routines were in constant evolution, as workers learned how to manipulate and alter each stage of the labor process. More largely, the "rhythm" of work means that by repeating a particular operation, we find how to speed up and slow down, make variations, play with materials, develop new practices—just as a musician learns how to manage time in performing a piece of music. Thanks to repetition and rhythm, the worker can achieve, Diderot said, "the unity of mind and hand" in labor.[12]

Of course, this is an ideal. Diderot offers evidence of a visual and subtle kind to make it convincing. At the paper mill the young boys cutting up rancid rags are shown working alone in a room, without an adult overseer. In the sizing, drying, and finishing rooms, young boys, young women, and burly men work side by side; here the *Encyclopedia*'s audience literally saw equality and fraternity. What makes that imagery specially compelling visually is the faces of the workers. No matter how demanding the tasks engaging them, the workers' faces are serene, reflecting Diderot's conviction that through labor human beings come to be at peace with themselves. "Let's work without theorizing," Martin says in Voltaire's *Candide.* "It's the only way to make life bearable." Though Diderot was more inclined to theorize, like Voltaire he believed that through mastering routine and its rhythms, people both take control and calm down.

TO ADAM SMITH, these images of orderly evolution, fraternity, and serenity represent an impossible dream. Routine deadens the spirit. Routine, at least as organized in the emerging capitalism which he observed, seemed to deny any connection between ordinary labor and the positive role of repetition in making art. When Adam Smith published *The Wealth of Nations* in 1776, he was read—as he has continued to be read— as an apostle of that new capitalism. This was because of the declaration he made at the outset of his book in favor of free markets. But Smith is more than an apostle of economic liberty; he was fully aware of the dark side of the market. That awareness came to him particularly in considering the routine organization of time in this new economic order.

The Wealth of Nations is based on a single great insight: Smith believed the free circulation of money, goods, and labor would require people to do ever more specialized tasks. The growth of free markets is coupled to the division of labor in society. We easily understand Smith's idea of the division of labor in observing a beehive; as the hive grows in size, each of its cells becomes the site for a particular labor. Put formally, the numeric dimensions of exchange—be they size of the money supply or the quantity of goods in the market—are insepara- bly linked to specialization of productive function.

Smith's own graphic example is of a pin factory. (Not mod- ern sewing pins; eighteenth-century pins were the equivalent of our tacks and small nails, used in carpentry.) Smith calcu- lated a pin-maker doing everything for himself could make at most a few hundred pins a day; in a pin factory operating ac- cording to the new divisions of labor, where pin-making was broken down into all its component parts and each worker did only one of them, a pin-maker could process more than 16,000 pins a day.[13] The trade the pin factory engages in on the free market will only stimulate demand for pins, leading to larger enterprises, with ever more elaborate divisions of labor.

Like Diderot's paper mill, Smith's pin factory is a place to work but not to live in. The separation of home and labor is, Smith said, the most important of all the modern divisions of labor. And like Diderot's paper mill, Smith's pin factory oper- ates in an orderly fashion thanks to routine, each worker per- forming only one function. The pin factory differs from the paper mill in Smith's vision of how disastrous, humanly, it is to organize work time this way.

The world Smith lived in had, of course, been long familiar with routines and schedules of time. Church bells from the sixth century on had marked out time into religious units of the day; the Benedictines took an important step in the early Middle Ages by ringing bells to mark off the times for work and the times for eating as well as the times for prayer. Nearer to Smith's own day, mechanical clocks had replaced the bells of churches, and by the mid-eighteenth century pocket watches were in widespread use. Now mathematically precise time could be told wherever a person was, whether in earshot or eyesight of a church or not: time had thus ceased to be de- pendent on space. Why should extending this scheduling of time further prove a human disaster?

The Wealth of Nations is a very long book, and the propo- nents of the new economy in Smith's own time tended only to refer to its dramatic and hopeful beginning. As the text progresses, however, it darkens; the pin factory becomes a more sinister place. Smith recognizes that breaking the tasks involved in making pins down into their component parts would condemn individual pin-makers to a numbingly boring day, hour after hour spent doing one small job. At a certain point, routine becomes self-destructive, because human beings lose control over their own efforts; lack of control over work time means people go dead mentally.

The capitalism of his own time Smith believed was crossing this great divide; when Smith declares that "those who labor most get least" in the new order, he was thinking in these human terms, rather than about wages.[14] In one of the grimmest passages of *The Wealth of Nations* he writes:

> In the progress of the division of labour, the employment of the far greater part of those who live by labour . . . comes to be confined to a few very simple operations; frequently to one or two. . . . The man whose whole life is spent in performing a few simple operations . . . generally becomes as stupid and ignorant as it is possible for a human creature to become.[15]

The industrial worker thus knows nothing of the self-possession and mobile expressiveness of the actor who has memorized a thousand lines; Diderot's comparison of actor and worker is false, because the worker does not control his or her work. The pin-maker becomes a "stupid and ignorant" creature in the course of the division of labor; the repetitive nature of his work has pacified him. For these reasons, industrial routine threatens to diminish human character in its very depths.

If this seems a strangely pessimistic Adam Smith, it is perhaps only because he was a more complex thinker than capitalist ideology makes him out to be. In *The Theory of Moral Sentiments* he had earlier argued for the virtues of mutual sympathy and the capacity to identify with the needs of others. Sympathy, he argued, is a spontaneous moral sentiment; it bursts forth suddenly when a man or woman suddenly understands the sufferings or stresses of another. The division of labor dulls, however, spontaneous outburst; routine represses the pouring forth of sympathy. To be sure, Smith equated the growth of markets and the division of labor with the material progress of society, but not with its moral progress. And the virtues of sympathy reveal something perhaps more subtle about individual character.

Rico's moral center, as we have seen, lay in the resolute assertion of his will; for Smith, the spontaneous eruption of sympathy overcomes the will, sweeps a man or woman up in emotions beyond his or her control, like sudden identification with society's failures, compassion for habitual liars or for cowards. Eruptions of sympathy—this realm of spontaneous time—pushes us outside our normal moral boundaries. There is nothing predictable or routine about sympathy.

In emphasizing the ethical importance of such bursts of emotion, Smith spoke distinctively among his contemporaries. Many of them viewed human character, in its ethical aspect, as having little to do with spontaneous feeling, or indeed with human will; Jefferson declared in the *Bill for Establishing Religious Freedom* (1779), that "the opinions and beliefs of men depend not on their own will, but follow involuntarily the evidence proposed to their own minds."[16] Character turns on doing one's duty; as James Madison said in 1785, following the dictates of conscience "is unalienable also, because what is here a right towards men, is a duty towards the Creator."[17] Nature and Nature's God proposes; man obeys.

Adam Smith speaks a language of character which is perhaps closer to our own. Character appears to him shaped by history and its unpredictable twists. Once established, a routine doesn't permit much in the way of personal history; to develop one's character, one has to break out of routine. This general proposition Smith made specific; he celebrated the character of traders, believing they acted responsively and sympathetically to the changing demands of the moment, just as he pitied the state of character of industrial workers yoked to routine. The trader was, in his view, the more fully engaged human being.

It should not surprise us that Marx was a close reader of Adam Smith, though hardly a celebrant of trade or traders. As a young man, Marx admired at least the general theory of spontaneity in *The Theory of Moral Sentiments*; as a more adult and sober analyst, he zeroed in upon Smith's depiction of the ills of routine, the division of labor without the worker's control of work—these are the essential ingredients of Marx's analysis of commodified time. Marx added to Smith's depiction of routine in the pin factory the contrast to such older practices as the German system of *Tagwerk,* in which a laborer was paid by the day; in that practice, the worker could adapt to the conditions of his or her environment, working differently on days when it rained than on clear days, or organizing tasks to take account of the delivery of supplies; there was rhythm to such work, because the worker was in control.[18] By contrast, as the Marxist historian E. P. Thompson would later write, in modern capitalism those employed "experience a distinction between their employer's time and their 'own' time."[19]

The fears Adam Smith and Marx harbored of routine time passed into our own century as the phenomenon called Fordism. It's in Fordism that we can most fully document the apprehension Smith had about the industrial capitalism just emerging at the end of the eighteenth century, particularly in the place for which Fordism was named.

THE FORD MOTOR COMPANY'S Highland Park factory was generally considered, during the years 1910–14, to be an illustrious example of technologically based division of labor. Henry Ford was in some ways a humane employer; he gave workers good wages through a five-dollar-day pay scheme (the equivalent of $120 a day in 1997 dollars), and included workers in a profit-sharing plan. The operations on the factory floor were another matter. Henry Ford believed worry about the quality of work life "mere moonshine"; five dollars a day was a handsome enough reward for boredom.

Before Ford created model factories like Highland Park, the automobile industry was craft-based, with highly skilled workers doing many complex jobs on a motor or an auto body during the course of a working day. These workers enjoyed a great deal of autonomy, and the auto industry was in fact a cluster of decentralized shops. "Many skilled workers," Stephan Meyer notes, "often hired and fired their own helpers and paid the latter some fixed proportion of their earnings."[20] Around 1910, the pin-maker's regime took hold in the auto industry.

As Ford Motor industrialized its production process, it favored the employment of so-called specialist workers over skilled craftsmen; the jobs of the specialist workers were those sorts of miniature operations requiring little thought or judgment. In the Ford plant at Highland Park, most of these specialist workers were recent immigrants, while the skilled craftsmen consisted of Germans and other more established Americans; the new immigrants were thought both by management and the "native" Americans to lack the intelligence to do more than routine work. By 1917, 55 percent of the work force were specialist employees; another 15 percent were unskilled cleaners and janitors hovering on the sidelines of the assembly line, and the crafts and technical workers had fallen to 15 percent.

"Cheap men need expensive jigs," said Sterling Bunnell, an early proponent of these changes, while "highly skilled men need little outside of their tool chests."[21] That insight about using complicated machinery to simplify human labor laid the foundation for the consummation of Smith's fears. For instance, the industrial psychologist Frederick W. Taylor believed that machinery and industrial design could be immensely complicated in a great enterprise, but there was no need for the workers to understand that complexity; indeed, he asserted, the less they were "distracted" by understanding the design of the whole, the more efficiently they would stick to doing their own jobs.[22] Taylor's infamous time-motion studies were conducted with a stopwatch, measuring to the fraction of a second how long installing a head-lamp or a fender should take. Time-motion management carried Smith's image of the pin factory to a sadistic extreme, but

Taylor had little doubt his human guinea pigs would passively accept measurement and manipulation.

In fact, passive acceptance of this routine time-slavery did not follow as a consequence; David Noble observes that "workers displayed a wide repertoire of techniques for sabotaging time-motion studies and, as a matter of course, ignored methods and process specifications whenever they got in the way or conflicted with their own interests."[23] Moreover, Smith's "stupid and ignorant" creature became depressed at work, and this diminished his or her productivity. Experiments like those at Western Electric's Hawthorn plant showed that nearly any attention paid to workers as sentient human beings improved their productiveness; industrial psychologists like Elton Mayo thus urged managers to show more concern for their employees and adapted psychiatric practices of counseling to the workplace. Still, industrial psychologists like Mayo were clear-eyed. They knew they could temper the pains of boredom, but not erase them in this iron cage of time.

The pains of routine culminated in Enrico's generation. In a classic study of the 1950s, "Work and Its Discontents," Daniel Bell sought to analyze this apotheosis in another automobile site, the General Motors Willow Run plant in Michigan. Smith's honeycomb had now become truly gigantic; Willow Run was a structure two-thirds of a mile long and a quarter of a mile wide. Here all the materials needed to make cars, from raw steel to glass blocks to leather tanneries, were assembled under a single roof, the work coordinated by a highly disciplined bureaucracy of analysts and managers. So complex an organization could function only via precise rules, which Bell called an "engineering rationality." This immense, well-engineered cage operated on three principles: "the logic of size, the logic of 'metric time,' and the logic of hierarchy."[24]

The logic of size was simple: bigger is more efficient. Concentrating all elements of production in one place like Willow Run conserved energy, saved on the transport of materials, and meshed the factory with the company's white-collar sales and executive offices.

The logic of hierarchy was not quite so simple. Max Weber had asserted in defining the human iron cage that "no special proof is necessary to show that military discipline is the ideal model for the modern capitalism factory."[25] In companies like General Motors in the 1950s, however, Bell noted a somewhat different model of control. The "superstructure which organizes and directs production . . . draws all possible brainwork away from the shop; everything is centered in the planning and schedule and design departments." Architecturally, this meant removing the technicians and managers as far from the throbbing machinery of the plants as possible. The generals of work thus lost physical contact with their troops. The result, however, only reinforced the numbing evils of routine for "the worker at the bottom, attending only to details, [who] is divorced from any decision or modification about the product he is working on."[26]

These ills at Willow Run continued to be founded on the Taylorite logic of "metric time." Time was minutely calculated everywhere in the vast plant so that top managers knew precisely what everyone was supposed to be doing at a given moment. Bell was struck, for instance, by how General Motors "divides the hour into ten six-minute periods . . . the worker is paid by the numbers of tenths of an hour he works."[27] This minute engineering of work time was connected to very long measures of time in the corporation as well. Seniority pay was finely tuned to the total number of hours a man or woman had worked for General Motors; a laborer could minutely calculate benefits of vacation time and sick leave. The micrometrics of time governed the lower echelons of white-collar offices as well as manual labor on the assembly line, in terms of promotion and benefits.

By Enrico's generation, however, metrics of time had become something other than an act of repression and domination practiced by management for the sake of the giant industrial organization's growth. Intense negotiations over these schedules preoccupied both the United Auto Workers union and the management of General Motors; the rank and file in the union paid close and at times passionate attention to the numbers involved in these negotiations. Routinized time had become an arena in which workers could assert their own demands, an arena of empowerment.

This was a political outcome Adam Smith did not anticipate. The entrepreneurial storms which Schumpeter summoned in the image of "creative destruction" meant that Smith's kind of pin factory went bankrupt throughout the nineteenth century, its rational honeycomb a design on paper which survived in metal and stone often only for a few years. Correspondingly, to preserve themselves against these upheavals, workers sought to routinize time, through savings in mutual aide societies, or through mortgages on homes gained through building societies. We are hardly disposed now to think of routinized time as a personal *achievement*, but given the stresses, booms, and depressions of industrial capitalism, it often became so. This complicated the meaning of the engineering of routine time which appeared at Ford's Highland Park and found a consummation of sorts in General Motors' Willow Run. We have seen how, out of this obsessive attention to the routine schedules of time, Enrico crafted a positive narrative for his life. Routine can demean, but it can also protect; routine can decompose labor, but it can also compose a life.

Still, the substance of Smith's fear remained vivid to Daniel Bell, who was then still trying to make sense of why workers did not revolt against capitalism. Bell was, as it were, halfway out of the door of socialist faith. He had learned that the discontents of work, even those as profound as the hollowing out of the content of work, do not lead men and women to revolt: resistance to routine does not beget revolution. But still Bell remained a good son in the socialist house. He believed that at the sprawling Willow Run factory he had visited the scene of a tragedy.

A thread connected Bell's Willow Run back in time to Ford's Highland Park and then again to Adam Smith's pin factory.

Routine has appeared in all these scenes of labor as personally degrading, a source of mental ignorance—and ignorance of a particular kind. The immediate present may be clear enough, as a laborer presses the same lever or crank hour after hour. What the routine worker lacks is any larger vision of a different future, or knowledge about how to make change. To rephrase this criticism of routine, mechanical activity does not beget any sense of a larger historical narrative: the micronarratives in the lives of workers like Enrico would have appeared to Marx negligible on the larger scale of History, or mere accommodations to existing circumstances.

This is why the old debate between Denis Diderot and Adam Smith remains vividly alive. Diderot did not believe routine work is degrading; on the contrary, he thought routines beget narratives, as the rules and rhythms of work gradually evolve. It's ironic that this boulevardier and *philosophe,* a creature of the sleazier salons of mid-eighteenth-century Paris, appears today more a champion of the inherent dignity of ordinary labor than do many of those who have spoken in the name of the People. Diderot's greatest modern heir, the sociologist Anthony Giddens, has tried to keep Diderot's insight alive by pointing to the primary value of habit in both social practices and self-understanding; we test out alternatives only in relation to habits which we have already mastered. To imagine a life of momentary impulses, of short-term action, devoid of sustainable routines, a life without habits, is to imagine indeed a mindless existence.[28]

Today we stand at a historical divide on the issue of routine. The new language of flexibility implies that routine is dying in the dynamic sectors of the economy. However, most labor remains inscribed within the circle of Fordism. Simple statistics are hard to come by, but a good estimate of the modern jobs described in Table 1 is that at least two-thirds are repetitive in ways which Adam Smith would recognize as akin to those in his pin factory. The computer use at work portrayed in Table 7 similarly involves, for the most part, quite routine tasks like data entry. If we believe, with Diderot and Giddens, that such labor need not be inherently demeaning, then we would focus on the working conditions in which it gets done; we would hope to make factories and offices look more like the cooperative, supportive scenes of labor depicted in the engravings of L'Anglée.

If, however, we are disposed to view routine as inherently demeaning, then we will attack the very nature of the work process itself. We will abhor both routine and its father, the dead hand of bureaucracy. We may be largely driven by the practical desire for greater market responsiveness, productivity, and profit. But we need not be just greedy capitalists; we may believe, as heirs of Adam Smith, that people are stimulated by more flexible experience, both at work and in other institutions. We may believe in the virtues of spontaneity. The question then becomes: will flexibility with all the risks and uncertainties it entails in fact remedy the human evil it sets out to attack? Even supposing routine has a pacifying effect on character, just how is flexibility to make a more engaged human being?

THREE
Flexible

The word "flexibility" entered the English language in the fifteenth century. Its meaning originally derived from the simple observation that though a tree may bend in the wind, its branches spring back to their original position. "Flexibility" names the tree's capacity both to yield and to recover, both the testing and the restoration of its form. Ideally, flexible human behavior ought to have the same tensile strength: adaptable to changing circumstances yet not broken by them. Society today is searching for ways to destroy the evils of routine through creating more flexible institutions. The practices of flexibility, however, focus mostly on the forces bending people.

Early modern philosophers equated the bending aspect of flexibility with the self's powers of sensation. Locke, in his *Essay Concerning Human Understanding,* wrote: "Self is that conscious thinking thing . . . which is sensible or conscious of pleasure and pain, capable of happiness or misery. . . ." Hume, in *A Treatise of Human Nature,* asserted that "when I enter most intimately into what I call *myself,* I always stumble on some particular perception or other, of heat or cold, light or shade, love or hatred, pain or pleasure."[29] These sensations come from stimuli in the world outside, which bend the self now one way, now another. Smith's theory of moral sentiments was founded on these external, changing stimuli.

Philosophical thinking about character struggled thereafter to find principles of inner regulation and recovery which would rescue the sense of oneself from sensory flux. In writings after Adam Smith devoted to political economy, however, the emphasis was put on sheer change. Flexibility of this sort was associated with the entrepreneurial virtues; following Smith, political economists in the nineteenth century opposed the entrepreneur's agility to the industrial laborer's dull plodding; John Stuart Mill, in his *Principles of Political Economy,* looked at markets as a theater of life both dangerous and challenging, and at its traders as artists of improvisation.

Whereas Adam Smith was a moralist of sympathy, the political economists who followed him focused on a different ethical value. To Mill, flexible behavior begets personal freedom. We are still disposed to think it does; we imagine being open to change, being adaptable, as qualities of character needed for free action—the human being free because capable of change. In our own time, however, the new political economy betrays this personal desire for freedom. Revulsion against bureaucratic routine and pursuit of flexibility has produced new structures of power and control, rather than created the conditions which set us free.

THE SYSTEM OF POWER which lurks in modern forms of flexibility consists of three elements: discontinuous reinvention of institutions; flexible specialization of production; and concentration of without centralization of power. The facts which fall under each of these categories are familiar to most of us, rather than arcane; it is harder to assess the personal consequences of these facts.

Discontinuous reinvention of institutions. Business manuals and magazines today tend to portray flexible behavior as requiring the desire for change; but in fact it is change of a particular sort, with particular consequences for our sense of time. The anthropologist Edmund Leach has sought to divide the experience of changing time into two sorts. In one, we know things change, but they seem to have a continuity with what came before. In the other, there is rupture because of acts which have irreversibly altered our lives. [30]

Consider, for example, a religious ritual like Communion. When you take the wafer you join in the same act performed by someone two hundred years ago. If you substitute brown-wheat wafers for white wafers you don't greatly disturb the meaning of the ritual; the new flour is incorporated in the rite. But if you insist that married women be allowed as priests to officiate at Communion, you may cause the very meaning of "priest" to change irreversibly, and so the meaning of Communion.

In the sphere of labor, the rhythms Diderot depicted in the paper mill or the habits portrayed by Anthony Giddens exemplify the first sense of changing but continuous time. By contrast, flexible change, of the sort which takes aim today at bureaucratic routine, seeks to reinvent institutions decisively and irrevocably, so that the present becomes discontinuous from the past.

The cornerstone of modern management practice is the belief that loose networks are more open to decisive reinvention than are pyramidal hierarchies such as ruled the Fordist era. The join between nodes in the network is looser; you can take away a part, at least in theory, without destroying other parts. The system is fragmented; therein lies the opportunity for intervening. Its very incoherence invites your revisions.

The specific techniques for reinventing institutions in this way are by now well worked out. Managers make use of software programs which standardize operational procedures (SIMS); it is possible for a very large corporation to see what all the cells in its institutional honeycomb are producing by using SIMS software, and so cut out duplication or ineffectual units quickly. These same software maquettes make it possible for accountants and institutional planners to assess quantitatively what programs or personnel can be cut in a merger of corporations. "Delayering" refers to the specific practice of giving a smaller number of managers control over a greater number of subordinates; "vertical disaggregation" gives members of a corporate island many multiple tasks to perform.

The familiar term for such practices is "reengineering," and the most salient fact about reengineering is the downsizing of jobs. Estimates of the numbers of American workers who have been downsized from 1980 to 1995 varied from a low count of 13 million to as high as 39 million. Downsizing has had a direct connection to growing inequality, since only a minority of the middle-aged workers squeezed out have found replacement labor at the same or higher wages. In a modern bible on this subject, *Re-engineering the Corporation,* the authors, Michael Hammer and James Champy, defend organizational reengineering against the charge that it is a mere cover for firing people by asserting that "downsizing and restructuring only mean doing less with less. Reengineering, by contrast, means doing *more* with less."[31] This declaration invokes efficiency—the very word "reengineering" conjures up a tighter operation achieved by making a decisive break with the past. But the overtones of efficiency reengineering are misleading. Irreversible change occurs precisely because reengineering can be a highly chaotic process.

It became clear to many business leaders by the mid-1990s, for instance, that only in the highly paid fantasy life of consultants can a large organization define a new business plan, trim and "reengineer" itself to suit, then steam forward to realize the new design. Erik Clemons, one of the most sober and practical of these consultants, observed self-critically that "many, even most, reengineering efforts fail," largely because institutions become dysfunctional during the people-squeezing process: business plans are discarded and revised; expected benefits turn out to be ephemeral; the organization loses direction.[32] Institutional changes, instead of following the path of a guided arrow, head in different and often conflicting directions: a profitable operating unit is suddenly sold, for example, yet a few years later the parent company tries to get back into the business in which it knew how to make money before it sought to reinvent itself. Such twists have prompted

the sociologists Scott Lash and John Urry to speak more largely of flexibility as "the end of organized capitalism."[33]

The phrase may seem extreme. Still, because managerial
ideology presents the drive for institutional change as a matter
of achieving greater efficiency rather than conducting an
open-ended experiment, we need to ask if it has succeeded.
Specifically, the new regime has taken aim at the evils of routine in the name of greater productivity.

In the early 1990s the American Management Association
and the Wyatt Companies conducted studies of firms which
had engaged seriously in downsizing. The AMA found that repeated downsizings produce "lower profits and declining
worker productivity"; the Wyatt study found that "less than
half the companies achieved their expense reduction goals;
fewer than one-third increased profitability" and less than one
in four increased their productivity.[34] The reasons for this failure were in part self-evident: the morale and motivation of
workers dropped sharply in the various squeeze plays of
downsizing. Surviving workers waited for the next blow of the
ax rather than exulting in competitive victory over those who
were fired.

More generally, though large-scale measures of productivity
are endlessly complex, there are at least good grounds for
doubt that the present era is more productive than the recent
past. Consider, for instance, a specific measure of growth,
gross domestic product. By this measure, growth was greater
in the era of the bureaucratic dinosaurs; the rates of productivity have slowed in all major industrial societies. (Please see
Table 3.) Because of advances in technology, there has been a
significant increase in the manufacturing sector of some countries. But reckoning in all forms of white-collar as well as blue-
collar labor, productivity has slowed overall, measured either
in terms of the output of individual workers or in terms of the
working hour. Some economists have even argued that when
all the costs of computerizing work are added up, technology
has actually shown a productivity deficit.[35]

Inefficiency or disorganization does not mean, however, that there is no rhyme or reason to the practice of sharp, disruptive change. Such institution reorganizations signal that change is for real, and as we know only too well, the stock prices of institutions in the course of reorganization thereby often rise, as though any change is better than continuing on as before. In the operation of modern markets, disruption of organizations has become profitable. While disruption may not be justifiable in terms of productivity, the short-term returns to stockholders provide a strong incentive to the powers of chaos disguised by that seemingly assuring word "reengineering." Perfectly viable businesses are gutted or abandoned, capable employees are set adrift rather than rewarded, simply because the organization must prove to the market that it is capable of change.

But there are more fundamental reasons driving modern capitalism to seek for change of a decisive, irreversible sort, disorganized or unproductive as it may be. These have to do with the volatility of consumer demand. This volatility of demand produces a second characteristic of flexible regimes, flexible specialization of production.

Flexible specialization. Put simply, flexible specialization tries to get more varied products ever more quickly to market. In *The Second Industrial Divide*, the economists Michael Piore and Charles Sabel describe how flexible specialization works in the supple relations between smallish firms in northern Italy, allowing these businesses to respond quickly to changes in consumer demand. The firms both cooperate and compete, searching for market niches which each occupies temporarily rather than permanently, accommodating the short product life of clothing, or textiles, or machine parts. Government plays a positive role in helping these Italian firms innovate together rather than get locked into life-or-death battles. Piore and Sable call the system they studied "a strategy of permanent innovation: accommodation to ceaseless change, rather than an effort to control it."[36]

Flexible specialization is the antithesis of the system of production embodied in Fordism. Quite specifically; in the making of cars and trucks today, the old mile-long assembly line ob-

served by Daniel Bell has been replaced by islands of specialized production. Deborah Morales, who studied a variety of
these flexible plants in the auto industry, emphasizes how important is innovation in response to market demand in changing the weekly and sometimes the daily tasks workers are
asked to do.[37]

The ingredients necessary for flexible specialization are
again familiar to us. Flexible specialization suits high technology; thanks to the computer, industrial machines are easy to
reprogram and configure. The speed of modern communications has also favored flexible specialization, by making global market data instantly available to a company. Moreover,
this form of production requires quick decision-making, and
so suits the small work group; in a large bureaucratic pyramid, by contrast, decision-making can slow down as paper
rises to the top for approval from headquarters. The most
strongly flavored ingredient in this new productive process is
the willingness to let the shifting demands of the outside
world determine the inside structure of institutions. All these
elements of responsiveness make for an acceptance of decisive, disruptive change.

It may seem strange, at least to Americans, to draw an example of the leading edge of productive innovation from Italy.
Though both American and European firms have learned
much from Japanese techniques of flexible specialization,
American business rhetoric often assumes that the American
economy is on the whole more flexible than other economies,
because of greater freedom from government interference in
this country than in Europe and Japan, a weaker old-boy network, weaker unions, and a public willing to tolerate disruptive economic change. (Please see Table 10.)

This American prejudice is founded on an implicit recognition that the flexible regime is political as well as economic.
Questions about flexibility address matters of political economy proper, and do find contrasting formulations today in
America and in parts of Europe. Are there any limits to how

much people are forced to bend? Can government give people something like the tensile strength of a tree, so that individuals do not break under the force of change?

The French banker Michel Albert draws out the contrast between answers by dividing the political economies of the advanced nations into a "Rhine" model and an "Anglo-American" model. The first has existed for nearly a century in the Netherlands, Germany, and France: in it labor unions and management share power, and the welfare apparatus of the government provides a comparatively tightly woven safety net of pensions, education, and health benefits. This Rhine model has served Italy, Japan, Scandinavia, and Israel as well.

The other model, the "Anglo-American," refers to the condition of Great Britain and America today, rather than to the past. This model gives free-market capitalism greater scope. While the Rhine model emphasizes certain obligations of economic institutions to the polity, the Anglo-American model stresses the state bureaucracy's subordination to the economy, and thus is willing to loosen the safety net provided by government.[38]

The Rhine model can behave as flexibly and decisively as the Anglo-American in terms of markets. Northern Italy, for instance, is quite "Rhinish" in its mix of government and private enterprise and also flexible in responding quickly and adeptly to changing market demand. In some forms of high-tech manufacturing, the thick Rhinish network of shifting associations can indeed be more responsive to consumer demand than its neoliberal cousin locked in dubious battle against government "interference" and bent on annihilating its competitors. The relation between the market and the state makes for the real difference between the two regimes.

The Rhine regimes tend to put the brakes on change when their less powerful citizens suffer, while the Anglo-American regime is more inclined to pursue changes in work organizations and practices even though the weak might pay a price. The Rhine model is somewhat friendly to government bu-

reaucracy, while the Anglo-American operates on the principle that government is guilty until proven innocent. Ruud
Lubbers, the former prime minister of the Netherlands, has
argued that the Dutch trust in the government has indeed
made possible painful economic adjustments which a more
adversarial citizenry would not have accepted.[39] Thus, the
label "neoliberalism" is often applied to the Anglo-American
model ("liberal" in its root sense of unregulated); "state capitalism" is applied to the Rhine.

These regimes have different defects. The Anglo-American
regime has had low unemployment but increasing wage inequality. The brute facts of current wealth inequality in the
Anglo-American regime are indeed staggering. The economist
Simon Head has calculated that for the bottom 80 percent of the
American working population, average weekly wages (adjusted
for inflation) fell by 18 percent from 1973 to 1995, while the pay
of the corporate elite rose 19 percent before taxes, and 66 percent after the tax accountants had worked their magic.[40] Another
economist, Paul Krugman, argues that the top 1 percent of
American wage-earners more than doubled their real incomes in
the decade 1979–89, in comparison to a much lower rate of
wealth accumulated in the decades before.[41] In Britain, *The
Economist* recently calculated that the top 20 percent of the
working population earn seven times as much as the bottom 20
percent, while twenty years ago the spread was only four times.[42]
An American secretary of labor has thus argued, "We are on the
way to becoming a two-tiered society composed of a few winners
and a larger group left behind," a view seconded by the chairman
of the Federal Reserve Bank, who recently declared that unequal
income could become "a major threat to our society."[43]

While in the Rhine regimes the gap in wage wealth has not
grown as much in the last generation, unemployment has become a curse. During three years, between 1993 and 1996, the
American economy generated nearly 8.6 million jobs, and
from 1992 on the British job market also began to flourish,
while during the last decade almost all of the continental and
Japanese labor market stagnated.[44] (Please see Table 2.)

Drawing out these differences emphasizes a simple fact. The operation of flexible production depends on how a society defines the common good. The Anglo-American regime has few political restraints on wealth inequality but full employment, while the welfare networks of the Rhinish states, which are more sensitive to ordinary workers, are a drag on job creation. Which evil you tolerate depends on which good you pursue. It's for this reason that the word "regime" is useful; it suggests the terms of power on which markets and production are allowed to operate.

Concentration without centralization. A flexible regime has a third characteristic. The changes in networks, markets, and production it utilizes permit what seems an oxymoron, the concentration of power without centralization of power.

One of the claims made for the new organization of work is that it decentralizes power, that is, gives people in the lower ranks of organizations more control over their own activities. Certainly this claim is false in terms of the techniques employed for taking apart the old bureaucratic behemoths. The new information systems provide a comprehensive picture of the organization to top managers in ways which give individuals anywhere in the network little room to hide; SIMS replaces the negotiations that might protect individuals in dealing only with their immediate superiors. Similarly, vertical disaggregation and delayering are anything but decentralizing procedures. There is a mainland of power in the archipelago of flexible power; someone on the mainland decides that "Barbados" can do the jobs once done on "Trinidad" and "Guadeloupe"; "Barbados" seldom chooses to add to its own burdens.

The managerial overburdening of small work groups with many diverse tasks is a frequent feature of corporate reorganization—and contrary to the ever finer divisions of labor Adam Smith imagined in the pin factory. To make such experiments with tens or hundreds of thousands of employees requires immense powers of command. To the economics of inequality the new order thus adds new forms of unequal, arbitrary power within the organization.

In terms of flexible specialization, consider the brand-name personal computers we buy; they are a collage of parts and partial assemblies made all over the world, the brand name representing at most a final framing of the whole. Their production occurs in a global labor market and results in a productive practice called "hollowing," since the brand name is a hollow sign. In his classic study *Lean and Mean*, Bennett Harrison shows just how hierarchical power remains firmly in place in this kind of production; the large corporation holds the shifting *corps de ballet* of dependent firms in its grip, passing on dips in the business cycle or product flops to its weaker partners, which are squeezed harder. The islands of work lie offshore of a mainland of power.

Harrison calls this network of unequal and unstable relations "concentration without centralization"; it complements the power to reorganize an institution top-down into fragments and nodes in a network. Control can be exercised by setting production or profit targets for a wide variety of groups in the organization, which each unit is free to meet in any way that seems fit. This freedom is, however, specious. It's rare for flexible organizations to set easily met goals; usually the units are pressed to produce or to earn far more than lies within their immediate capabilities. The realities of supply and demand are seldom in sync with these targets; the effort is to push units harder and harder despite those realities, a push which comes from the institution's top management.[45]

Another way to understand the power system described by Harrison is to say that challenging the old bureaucratic order has not meant *less* institutional structure. The structure remains in the forces driving units or individuals to achieve; what is left open is how to do so, and the flexible organization's top seldom provides the answers. It is more in the position of doing the accounting on its own demands, rather than designing a system by which the demands can be carried out. "Concentration without centralization" is a way of conveying the operation of command in a structure which no longer has the clarity of a pyramid—the institutional structure has become more convoluted, not simpler. This is why the very word "debureaucratization" is misleading as well as ungainly. In modern organizations which practice concentration without centralization, domination from the top is both strong and shapeless.

ONE WAY TO UNDERSTAND the way the three elements of the flexible regime join together is in the organization of time in the workplace. Flexible organizations today are experimenting with varying schedules of time called "flextime." Instead of fixed shifts unchanging from month to month, the working day is a mosaic of people working on different, more individualized schedules, as in Jeannette's office. This mosaic of working time seems far from the monotonous organization of labor in the pin factory; indeed, it seems a liberation of working time, a true benefit of the modern organization's attack on standardized routine. The realities of flextime are rather different.

Flextime arose from a new influx of women into the world of work. Poor women like Flavia have always worked in greater numbers than women of the bourgeoisie. In the last generation, as we have noted, significant numbers of women entered the ranks of middle-class labor in the United States, Europe, and Japan, and remained in the workforce even after bearing children; they joined the women who were already employed in lower-level service and manufacturing jobs. In 1960, about 30 percent of American women were in the paid labor force and 70 percent were not; by 1990, nearly 60 percent were in the paid labor force and only 40 percent were not. In the developed economies of the world by 1990, nearly 50 percent of the professional and technical labor force had become composed of women, the majority employed full-time.[46] Necessity as well as personal desire has prompted this labor; a middle-class standard of life generally now requires two adult wage-earners. These women workers needed, however, more flexible working hours; in all classes, many of them are part-time workers and remain full-time parents. (Please see Table 5.)

The entry of more middle-class women into the labor force thus helped spur greater innovation in the flexible scheduling of full-time as well as part-time work. By now, these changes have crossed gender lines, so that men also have more plastic work schedules. Flextime today operates in several ways. The simplest, used in some way by about 70 percent of American corporations, is for a worker to put in a full work week but determine when during the day he or she is at the factory or office. At the opposite extreme, about 20 percent of the companies permit "compressed" work schedules, as when an employee does a full week's work in four days. Working at home is an option in about 16 percent of companies today, particularly for service, sales, and technical workers, made feasible in large part by the development of communications intranets. In the United States, white, middle-class men and women today have more access to flexible work schedules than factory operatives or Hispanic workers. Flextime is a privilege of the working day; work in the evening or at night still is passed on to the less privileged classes. (Please see Table 6.)

This fact flags one way in which flextime, though seeming to promise greater freedom than that of a worker yoked to the routine of Smith's pin factory, is woven instead into a new fabric of control. Flextime is not like the calendar of holidays in which workers know what to expect; nor is it comparable to the sheer total of weekly working hours which a corporation may set for its lower-level employees. Flexible scheduling of time is more a benefit conferred on favored employees, the management analyst Lotte Bailyn argues, than a working right; it is a benefit which is unequally apportioned and strictly rationed. This is now true in America; other countries are moving toward American practice.[47]

If flextime is an employee's reward, it also puts the employee in the institution's intimate grip. Take the most flexible of flextimes, working at home. This award arouses great anxiety among employers; they fear losing control over their absent workers and suspect that those who stay at home will abuse their freedom.[48] As a result, a host of controls have come into being to regulate the actual work processes of those who are absent from the office. People may be required to phone in to the office regularly, or intranet controls may be used to monitor the absent worker; e-mail is often opened by supervisors. Few organizations which deploy flextime propose to their workers, "Here is a task; do it any way you wish, so long as you get it done," on the *Tagwerk* model. A flextime worker controls the location of labor, but does not gain greater control over the labor process itself. By now, a number of studies suggest that the surveillance of labor is in fact often greater for those absent from the office than for those who are present.[49]

Workers thus exchange one form of submission to power—face-to-face—for another which is electronic; this is what Jeannette found, for instance, when moving to a more flexible workplace back East. The micromanagement of time proceeds apace, even as time seems deregulated in contrast to the evils of Smith's pin factory or Fordism. Daniel Bell's "metric logic" of time has shifted from the timeclock to the computer screen. Work is physically decentralized, power over the worker is more direct. Working at home is the ultimate island of the new regime.

THESE, THEN, ARE THE FORCES bending people to change: reinvention of bureaucracy, flexible specialization of production, concentration without centralization. In the revolt against routine, the appearance of a new freedom is deceptive. Time in institutions and for individuals has been unchained from the iron cage of the past, but subjected to new, top-down controls and surveillance. The time of flexibility is the time of a new power. Flexibility begets disorder, but not freedom from restraint.

Smith's Enlightenment version of flexibility imagined that it would enrich people ethically as well as materially; his flexible individual is capable of sudden bursts of sympathy for others. Quite a different character structure appears among those who exercise power within this complicated modern regime. They are free, but it is an amoral freedom.

FOR THE LAST FEW YEARS I've gone to a winter meeting of business and political leaders in the Swiss mountain resort of Davos. You reach the village up a narrow road through the Alps; Davos itself is laid out along one main street lined with hotels, shops, and ski chalets. Thomas Mann set *The Magic Mountain* here in a grand hotel which once served as a sanitarium for tuberculosis patients. For the one week of the World Economic Forum, Davos is home to power rather than health.

Along the main street a snake of limousines writhes in front of the conference hall, where there are guards, police dogs, and metal detectors. Each of the two thousand people who descend on the village need an electronic security badge to enter the hall, but the badge does more than keep out riffraff. It has an electronic code which allows the bearer to read and send messages on an elaborate computer system, and so to arrange meetings and to cut deals—in the coffee lounges, on the ski slopes, or at the exquisite dinners whose seating plans are frequently disrupted by the press of business.

Davos is devoted to global economic warming, the conference center filled with ex-communists extolling the virtues of free trade and conspicuous consumption. The lingua franca is English, signaling America's dominant role in the new capitalism, and most people here speak English extremely well. The World Economic Forum runs more like a court than a conference. Its monarchs are heads of big banks or international corporations, good at listening. The courtiers speak fluently and in a low key, pitching for loans or to make a sale. Davos costs businessmen (they are mostly men) a great deal of money, and only top people come. But the courtly atmosphere is infected with a certain fear, the fear of being "left out of the loop" even in this snowy Versailles.

A kind of familial bitterness has kept me coming back to Davos as an observer. My family were mostly American left-wing organizers. My father and uncle fought in the Spanish Civil War; originally they fought against the fascists in Spain, but by the end of the war they fought the communists as well. Disillusion following combat has been the story of the American left more largely. My own generation had to let go of the hopes which enthralled us in 1968, when revolution seemed just around the corner; most of us have come to rest uneasily in that nebulous zone just left of center, where high-flown words count for more than deeds.

And here on the ski slopes in Switzerland, dressed as if for sport, are the victors. I have learned one thing from my past: it would be fatal to treat them as merely perfidious. Whereas my kind has become adept at dwelling in a kind of passive suspicion of existing reality, the court of Davos is filled with energy. It speaks for great changes which have marked our time: new technologies, the attack on rigid bureaucracies, and transnational economics. Few of the people I've met at Davos began life as rich or powerful as they have become. This is a kingdom of achievers, and many of their achievements they owe to the practice of flexibility.

Davos Man is most publicly embodied in Bill Gates, the ubiquitous chairman of the Microsoft Corporation. He appeared recently, as do all main speakers at the gathering, both in person and blown up on a huge television screen. Mutterings were heard from some techies in the hall as the giant head spoke; they find the quality of Microsoft products mediocre. But to most of the executives, he is a heroic figure, and not just because he built a huge business from scratch. He is the very epitome of a flexible magnate, as shown most recently when he discovered that he had not foreseen the possibilities of the Internet. Gates turned his immense operations around on a dime, reorganizing his business focus in pursuit of the new market opportunity.

When I was a child, I had a set of books called the Little Lenin Library which set out in graphic detail the character of self-made capitalists. A particularly grisly picture showed the elder John D. Rockefeller as an elephant crushing hapless workers beneath his huge feet, his trunk grasping train engines and oil derricks. Ruthless and greedy Davos Man may be, but those animal qualities alone are not enough to account for the character traits of the technology moguls, venture capitalists, and experts in company reengineering assembled here.

Gates, for instance, seems free of the obsession to hold on to things. His products are furious in coming forth and as rapid in disappearing, whereas Rockefeller wanted to own oil rigs, buildings, machinery, or railroads for the long term. Lack of long-term attachment seems to mark Gates's attitude toward work: he spoke about positioning oneself in a network of possibilities rather than paralyzing oneself in one particular job. By all accounts he is a ruthless competitor, and the evidence of his greed is a matter of public record; he has devoted only a minuscule slice of his billions to charity or to the public good. But the disposition to bend is evinced by his willingness to destroy what he has made, given the demands of the immediate moment—he has the ability to let go, if not to give.

This lack of temporal attachment is connected to a second character trait of flexibility, the tolerance for fragmentation. When Gates lectured last year, he offered a particular piece of advice. He counseled us in the hall that the growth of technology businesses is a messy affair, marked by many experiments, wrong turns, and contradictions. Other American techies made the same point to their Rhine-European colleagues, who, seemingly stuck in old formalistic ways, want to devise a coherent "technology policy" for their companies or their countries. Growth, the Americans said, doesn't happen in that neat, bureaucratically planned way.

It may be no more than economic necessity which today drives the capitalist to pursue many possibilities at the same time. Such practical realities require, however, a particular strength of character—that of someone who has the confidence to dwell in disorder, someone who flourishes in the midst of dislocation. Rico, as we have seen, suffered emotionally from the social displacements which came with his success. The true victors do not suffer from fragmentation. Instead, they are stimulated by working on many different fronts at the same time; it is part of the energy of irreversible change.

The capacity to let go of one's past, the confidence to accept fragmentation: these are two traits of character which appear at Davos among people truly at home in the new capitalism. They are traits which encourage spontaneity, but here on the mountain such spontaneity is at best ethically neutral. These same traits of character begetting spontaneity become more self-destructive for those who work lower down in the flexible regime. The three elements of the system of flexible power corrode the characters of more ordinary employees who try to play by these rules. Or at least this is what I found in descending from the magic mountain and returning to Boston.

FOUR

Illegible

A year after Rico and I talked, I went back to the Boston bakery where twenty-five years ago, in researching *The Hidden Injuries of Class,* I had interviewed a group of bakers. I'd come originally to ask about their perceptions of class in America. Like almost all Americans they told me they were middle-class; at face value, the idea of social class signified little to them. Europeans from Tocqueville on have tended to take the face value for reality; some have deduced we Americans are indeed a classless society, at least in our manners and beliefs—a democracy of consumers; others, like Simone de Beauvoir, have maintained we are hopelessly confused about our real differences.

My interviewees a quarter century ago were not blind; they had a legible enough way of reckoning social class, though not the European way. Class involved a far more personal estimation of self and circumstance. Very sharp lines can be drawn between people in this way; the patrons of American fast-food restaurants, for instance, treat those who serve them with an indifference and rudeness which would be insulting and unacceptable in an English pub or French café. The masses seem not worth noticing as human beings, and so what matters is how much people stand out from the mass. The American obsession with individualism expresses the need for status on these terms; one wants to be respected for oneself. Class in America tends to be interpreted as an issue of personal character. And so when 80 percent of a group of bakers say, "I am middle-class," the real question being answered is not how rich are you or how powerful are you but how do you estimate yourself. The answer is, I am good enough.

Objective measures of social position such as Europeans reckon economically in terms of class are made by Americans more often in terms of race and ethnicity. At the time I first interviewed the Boston bakers, while the bakery had an Italian name and made Italian breads, most of the bakers were Greek; these Greeks were the sons of bakers who had worked for the same firm. For these Greek-Americans, "black" was a synonym for "poor," and "poor" became, via the alchemy which translated objective social standing into personal character, a cognate sign for "degraded." It enraged the people I interviewed at the time that the elite—that is, doctors, lawyers, professors, and other privileged whites—felt more for these supposedly lazy, dependent blacks than for the struggles of hardworking, independent-minded Americans in the middle. Racial hatred thus betrayed a class consciousness of sorts.

The Greek ethnicity of the bakers again helped them measure their own relatively low standing on the social scale. The Greeks made much of the fact that the managers of the bakery were indeed Italian. Many Boston Italians were as poor as other ethnic groups, but it was a commonplace in these other immigrant communities that Italians who had risen in society had help from the Mafia. The bakers worried about upward social mobility among themselves; they feared the children would lose their Greek roots in becoming more American. And the bakers were certain Boston's white Anglo-Saxon Protestants looked down on immigrant Americans like themselves—perhaps a realistic assessment.

The traditional Marxian approach to class consciousness is based on the labor process, specifically how workers relate to one another through their work. The bakery did bind its bakers self-consciously together. The place in one way more resembled Diderot's paper mill than Smith's pin factory, the baking of bread being a balletic exercise which required years of training to get right. Still, the bakery was filled with noise; the smell of yeast mingled with human sweat in the hot rooms; the bakers' hands were constantly plunged into flour and water; the men used their noses as well as their eyes to judge when the bread was done. Craft pride was strong, but the men said they didn't enjoy their work, and I believed them. The ovens often burned them; the primitive dough beater pulled human muscles; and it was night work, which meant these men, so family-centered, seldom saw their families during the week.

But it seemed to me, watching them struggle, that the ethnic solidarity of being Greek made possible their solidarity in this difficult labor—good worker meant good Greek. The equation of good work and good Greek made sense in the concrete, rather than the abstract. The bakers needed to cooperate intimately in order to coordinate the varied tasks of the bakery. When two of the bakers, brothers who were both alcoholic, showed up plastered on the job, others would berate them by referring to the mess they were making of their families and the loss of prestige of their families in the community where all the Greeks lived. Not being a good Greek was a potent tool of shame, and thus of work discipline.

Like Enrico, the Greek bakers in the Italian bakery had a set of bureaucratic guidelines to organize their experience for the long term. Bakery jobs had passed from their fathers to themselves via the local union, which also rigidly structured wages, benefits, and pensions. To be sure, the clarities in this bakers' world required certain fictions. The first owner of the bakery had been a very poor Jew, who made something of the business, then sold it to a medium-sized publicly traded organization which employed the managers with Italian surnames— but matters were clarified simply by equating Boss with Mafia. The union which organized their own lives was in fact a mess, some of its officials facing prison terms for corruption, the pension fund looted and depleted. Still, the bakers had told me, these corrupt union officers understood their needs.

These were some of the ways a group of workers made legible in a more personal language the conditions a European might read in terms of class. Race measured down; ethnicity measured up and "us." The character of the workers was expressed at work in acting honorably, working cooperatively and fairly with other bakers because they belonged to the same community.

When I returned to the bakery after talking to Rico, I was amazed at how much had changed.

A giant food conglomerate now owns the business, but this is no mass production operation. It works according to Piore and Sabel's principles of flexible specialization, using sophisticated, reconfigurable machines. One day the bakers might make a thousand loaves of French bread, the next a thousand bagels, depending on immediate market demand in Boston. The bakery no longer smells of sweat and is startlingly cool, whereas workers used frequently to throw up from the heat. Under the soothing fluorescent lights, all is now strangely silent.

Socially, this is no longer a Greek shop. All the men I'd known have retired; some young Italians now work here as bakers, along with two Vietnamese, an aging and incompetent WASP hippie, and several individuals without discernible ethnic identities. Moreover, the shop is no longer composed only of men; one of the Italians was a girl barely out of her teens, another woman has two grown children. Workers come and go throughout the day; the bakery is a tangled web of part-time schedules for the women and even a few of the men, the old night shift replaced by a much more flexible labor time. The power of the bakers' union has eroded in the shop; as a result, the younger people are not covered by union contracts, and they work on a contingent basis as well as on flexible schedules. Most strikingly, given the prejudices which ruled the old bakery, the shop-floor foreman is black.

From the vantage of the past, all these changes should be confusing. This bouillabaisse of ethnicity, gender, and race certainly makes it hard to read up and down in the old way. But the peculiarly American disposition to translate class into the more personal terms of status still prevails. What is truly new is that, in the bakery, I caught sight of a terrible paradox. In this high-tech, flexible work place where everything is user-friendly, the workers felt personally demeaned by the way they work. In this bakers' paradise, that reaction to their work is something they do not themselves understand. Operationally, everything is so clear; emotionally, so illegible.

Computerized baking has profoundly changed the balletic physical activities of the shop floor. Now the bakers make no physical contact with the materials or the loaves of bread, monitoring the entire process via on-screen icons which depict, for instance, images of bread color derived from data about the temperature and baking time of the ovens; few bakers actually see the loaves of bread they make. Their working screens are organized in the familiar Windows way; in one, icons for many more different kinds of bread appear than had been prepared in the past—Russian, Italian, French loaves all possible by touching the screen. Bread had become a screen representation.

As a result of working in this way, the bakers now no longer actually know how to bake bread. Automated bread is no marvel of technological perfection; the machines frequently tell the wrong story about the loaves rising within, for instance, failing to gauge accurately the strength of the rising yeast, or the actual color of the loaf. The workers can fool with the screen to correct somewhat for these defects; what they can't do is fix the machines, or more important, actually bake bread by manual control when the machines all too often go down. Program-dependent laborers, they can have no hands-on knowledge. The work is no longer legible to them, in the sense of understanding what they are doing.

The flexible time schedules in the bakery compound the difficulties of working this way. People often go home just as disaster is coming out of the oven. I don't mean the workers are irresponsible; rather, they have other demands on their time, children to tend, or other jobs where they must arrive on time. To deal with the computerized batches which misfire, it's easier now to chuck out the spoiled loaves, reprogram the computer, and start all over. In the old days, I saw very few waste scraps in the shop; now each day the huge plastic trash cans of the bakery are filled with mounds of blackened loaves. The trash cans seem apt symbols of what has happened to the art of baking. There's no necessary reason to romanticize this loss of human craft, though; as an avid amateur cook, I found the quality of the bread which survives the production process to be excellent, an opinion evidently shared by many Bostonians, since the bakery is popular and profitable.

According to old Marxian notions of class, the workers themselves should be alienated because of this loss of skill; they ought to be angry at the stupefying conditions of the workplace. The only person I could find in the bakery who fit this description, however, was the black foreman, who stood on the lowest rung of the management ladder.

Rodney Everts, as I will call him, is a Jamaican who came to Boston when he was ten and worked his way up in the old way, from apprentice to master baker to foreman. That trajectory represents twenty years of struggle. He was forced on the old management as part of a racial-equality ruling; he endured the daily coldness of the old Greeks, but made his way up through sheer determination and merit. Signs of struggle appear in his body; he is grossly overweight, an anxiety-driven eater; our talk at first revolved around yeast cultures and diets. Rodney Everts greeted the change of management as a release, since the new national company was less racist in character, and welcomed the technological changes in the bakery as lowering his own risk of a heart attack. He welcomed most of all the retirements of the Greeks and the hiring of the polyglot work- force. He is responsible, in fact, for choosing most of the peo- ple on the shop floor. But he is also angry at how blindly the workers work, even though he understands that the low level of solidarity and skill is not the workers' fault. Most of the peo- ple he chooses remain at most two years in the bakery; the young, nonunion workers are especially transitory. He is also angry at the company for preferring these nonunion workers; Everts is convinced that if they were better paid, they would stay longer. And he is angry at the company for using flextime schedules as a lure for low-wage work. He wants all his people together on the shop floor, at the same time, to deal with problems together as best they can. The overflowing trash cans infuriate him.

I warmed to Rodney Everts when he told me he believed many of these problems could be sorted out if the workers themselves owned the bakery. He is anything but passive in the face of the workers' inability to bake; he has given several voluntary seminars on the art of baking, attended only by the two Vietnamese, who can barely fathom his English. But I was most struck by his ability to stand back and look clearly. "When I apprenticed, you will understand, I had the blind rage of the black man"—a devout Bible reader, he has some of the King James cadences in his speech—"now I *see* this place." That clarity is what a humane Marx meant by alienation, the unhappy disassociated consciousness which reveals, however, things as they are and where a person stands.

But the foreman stands alone. The people beneath him do not see themselves in the same clear way. In place of alienation, their sense of daily life in the bakery was marked by indifference. For instance, in order to be hired now, the people on the shop floor have to prove they are computer-literate. However, they won't use much of this knowledge on the job, where they are simply pushing buttons in a Windows program designed by others. "Baking, shoemaking, printing, you name it, I've got the skills," said one of the women on the shop floor with a laugh as we stared at the trash cans. The bakers are vividly aware of the fact that they are performing simple, mindless tasks, doing less than they know how to do. One of the Italians said to me, "I go home, I really bake bread, I'm a baker. Here, I punch the buttons." When I asked him why he hadn't attended Everts's baking seminar, he replied, "it doesn't matter; I won't do this the rest of my life." Again and again, people said the same thing in different words: I'm not really a baker. Here are people whose work identities are weak. If Bill Gates is not much attached to specific products, this new generation is indifferent to specific labors.

But lack of attachment is also coupled with confusion. This polyglot flexible workforce had little more clarity about where they stood in the society. Racial and ethnic yardsticks are less useful to them than to the Greeks who worked here together before. They accepted the black Rodney Everts as a legitimate boss, his authority based on his real skill. The women in the bakery used the word "feminist" sourly. When I asked people the same question I'd posed twenty-five years before—"What class do you belong to?"—I got the same answer: the middle class. But now the old organizing subtexts were gone. (In making this generalization, I have to except the Vietnamese, with whom I had to speak in French; in their communal bonds they resembled the Greeks who had worked here before.)

Lack of attachment to particular tasks and confusion about social standing might be tolerable if there also had disappeared the peculiarly American disposition to translate material circumstances into questions of personal character. But that hasn't happened. Work experience still seems intensely personal. These people are powerfully driven to interpret their work as reflecting upon themselves as individuals. Twenty-five years ago I asked the Greek bakers, "What do you want to be respected for?" The answer was simple: being a good father, followed by a good worker. When I asked the twenty or so people in the bakery the same question on my return, sex and age complicated the family side of the answer, but, as before, being a good worker was still important. Now, though, in the flexible regime, the personal qualities of being a good worker seemed harder to define.

THE TECHNOLOGY IN THE BAKERY is relevant to that weak work identity, but not quite in the way one might expect. Rather than hostile, the machines in this workplace are all meant to be user-friendly; they have clear visual icons and well-organized windows which resemble home computer screens. A Vietnamese who barely speaks English and who has no real understanding of the difference between a baguette and a bagel can operate these machines. There is an economic rationale for these user-friendly mixers, kneaders, and ovens; they permitted the company to hire workers at lower wages than in the past, when the workers, not the machines, possessed skill—even though now all have higher formal technical qualifications.

It is, I came to realize, the very user-friendliness of the bakery that may account in part for the confusion the people baking feel about themselves as bakers. In all forms of work, from sculpting to serving meals, people identify with tasks which challenge them, tasks which are difficult. But in this flexible workplace, with its polyglot workers coming and going irregularly, radically different orders coming in each day, the machinery is the only real standard of order, and so has to be easy for anyone, no matter who, to operate. Difficulty is counterproductive in a flexible regime. By a terrible paradox, when we diminish difficulty and resistance, we create the very conditions for uncritical and indifferent activity on the part of the users.

In this regard, I was fortunate to be in the bakery when one of the dough-kneading machines blew up. Though simple to use, the dough-kneading machine was complex in design; its computer operating system was opaque, as industrial designers say, rather than transparent. "User-friendly" meant a rather one-sided version of friendliness. At the bakery that day, the electricity was shut off, a telephone call was made, and we sat for two hours waiting for the service saviors to arrive from the firm which had designed the machines.

Once the plug was pulled on the electricity, the waiting workers were morose and upset. This had happened before, but there was no way anyone on the shop floor could get into the opaque systems architecture to understand, much less solve, the problem. The bakers were not indifferent to the elemental fact of getting a job done. They wanted to be helpful, to make things work, but they couldn't. In a study of servers at McDonald's restaurants, Katherine Newman found that supposedly unskilled workers suddenly spring to mental attention and deploy all manner of improvised skills to keep the operation going when faced with a mechanical crisis like this.[50] The bakers felt this impulse to cope but were flummoxed by the technology.

It would, of course, be absurd to blame the machines. They were designed and built to work in a certain way; the company tolerated both wastage and breakdown as just part of the cost of doing business. At higher levels of technical work, the advent of the computer has enriched the content of many jobs. The far more positive side of technology appears, for instance, in the study made by Stanley Aronowitz and William DiFazio of the impact of auto-CAD, or computer-assisted design, on a group of civil engineers and architects working for the city of New York. People used to drawing by hand were excited by the possibility of manipulating images in a flexible way on screen. One architect told them, "At first I thought they would be just drafting machines . . . but I am really excited by it, it is like I can manipulate and take apart any drawing. I can stretch it, move it, take a piece out of it."[51] This use of the machine certainly has stimulated its high-level users to think.

Yet it would be equally wrong to exclude machinery from flexibility's detachment and confusions. This is because contemporary capitalism's new tool is a far more intelligent machine than the mechanical devices of the past. Its own intelligence can substitute for that of its users, and thus take Smith's nightmare of mindless labor to a new extremes. When CAD was first introduced into the architectural program of the Massachusetts Institute of Technology, for instance, one architect objected that

> when you draw a site, when you put in the counter lines and the trees, it becomes ingrained in your mind. You come to know the site in a way that is not possible with the computer. . . . You get to know a terrain by tracing and retracing it, not by letting the computer "regenerate" it for you.[52]

Similarly, the physicist Victor Weisskopf once said to students who worked exclusively with computerized experiments, "When you show me that result, the computer understands the answer, but I don't think you understand the answer."[53]

Like any act of thinking, intelligence in using machines is dull when operational rather than self-critical. The technology analyst Sherry Turkle recounts interviewing a highly intelligent young girl about how best to play SimCity, a computer city-planning game for children; one of the most effective rules was "Raising taxes always leads to riots."[54] The child did not question why raising taxes always leads to riots; she only knows this rule makes the game easy to play. In auto-CAD, you can plot on the machine a little bit of an object, and see almost immediately the whole thing; if you wonder what a scene would look like blown up, shrunk, reversed, from the back, then a few keystrokes will tell you. But it won't tell you if the image is any good.

The detachment and confusion I found among the bakers in Boston is a response to these peculiar properties of computer use in a flexible workplace. It wouldn't be news to any of these men and women that resistance and difficulty are important sources of mental stimulation, that when we struggle to know something, we know it well. But these truths have no home. Difficulty and flexibility are contraries in the bakery's ordinary productive process. At moments of breakdown, the bakers suddenly found themselves shut out from dealing with their work—and this rebounded to their sense of working self. When the woman in the bakery says "Baking, shoemaking, printing, you name it," her feel for the machine is of an easy, friendly sort. But she is also, as she repeated to me several times, no baker. These two statements are intimately linked. Her understanding of work is superficial; her identity as a worker is light.

It is a commonplace that modern identities are more fluid than the categorical divisions of people in the class-bound societies of the past. "Fluid" can mean adaptable. But in another train of associations, fluid also implies ease; fluid motion requires that there be no impediments. When things are made easy for us, as in the labor I've described, we become weak; our engagement with work becomes superficial, since we lack understanding of what we are doing.

Is not this the very same dilemma which worried Adam Smith? I believe not. Nothing was hidden from the worker in the pin factory; a great deal is hidden from the workers in the bakery. One's work is so clear yet so obscure. Flexibility creates distinctions between surface and depth; those who are flexibility's less powerful subjects are forced to remain on the surface.

The old Greek bakers had great physical difficulty doing their work—no one could wish for its return. Work was anything but superficial for them, because of their ethnic bonds—and in modern Boston those ties of communal honor are perhaps also gone for good. What matters now is what has taken their place, the association of the flexible and the fluid with the superficial. The glossy surfaces and simple messages which advertise global products are all too familiar, ever so consumer-friendly. But some of the same divide between surface and depth marks the flexible productive process, with its user-friendly tasks whose deeper logic cannot be cracked apart.

Just in the same way, people can suffer from superficiality in trying to read the world around them and read themselves. Images of a classless society, a common way of speaking, dressing, and seeing, can also serve to hide more profound differences; there is a surface on which everyone appears on an equal plane, but breaking the surface may require a code people lack. And if what people know about themselves is easy and immediate, it may be too little.

The opaque surfaces of work contrast with the enthusiasms of Davos. In the flexible regime, the difficulties crystallize in a particular act, the act of risk-taking.

FIVE

Risk

Until it closed, the Trout Bar was one of my favorite places to unwind in New York. Located in an old factory building in Soho, the Trout was not inviting; you walked down into a half-basement, and the view out the windows provided a democratic prospect of unidentifiable shoes and ankles. The Trout was Rose's kingdom.

She had, when barely out of high school, married well to a middle-aged felt manufacturer in the days when men wore hats. As was the way thirty years ago, she promptly had two babies. The felt manufacturer nearly as promptly died; the proceeds from his business she used to buy the Trout. Apparently you make your way in the bar business in New York either by becoming hot or remaining lukewarm; the first means snagging the floating population of models, bored rich, and media honchos who pass for "style" in our city, the second requires drawing in a sedentary local clientele. Rose chose the latter route as more certain and the Trout filled up.

Food at the Trout was only for the foolhardy. The cooks, Ernesto and Manolo, lacked any understanding of the function of heat in the cooking process, so that a rare cheeseburger usually arrived as a dry, leathery object requiring a sharp knife. But Ernesto and Manolo were Rose's "boys"; she joked with them, yelled at them, and they made rude comments back to her in Spanish. Out front, social life was different; people came there to be left alone. I suppose all big cities have oases like this. I saw the same regulars for an entire generation, and made endless conversation with them, without ever making friends.

Though in fact a solid, no-nonsense New Yorker, Rose looked and sounded like the "character" that people in New York Bohemia prefer. Her eyes were magnified by huge square glasses which only seemed to emphasize her voice, a nasal trumpet from which issued frequent cutting comments. Her actual character lay hidden behind this facade. She would have snorted had I ever told her she was sensitive and intelligent. But her problem was that she wasn't making anything of herself by serving coffee and drinks to the neighborhood's unemployed actors, tired writers, and beefy businessmen. She had the required midlife crisis.

A few years ago she decided to get out of the cozy, profitable realm she had constructed at the Trout. It was a logical moment to change; one of her daughters had married, the other had finally graduated from college. At various times, Rose had been canvassed for information by researchers for an advertising agency which specialized in beverages, merchandising booze in slick magazines. Now they told her about a two-year contract open in the agency for someone to work on revitalizing the sale of hard liquor, since the market share of scotch and bourbon was falling. Rose seized the opportunity, applied, and was accepted.

New York is the international home to the advertising trade, and people employed in the image business are easily spotted by other New Yorkers. Media men cultivate the look less of the staid official than of the prosperous artist: black silk shirts, black suits—a lot of expensive black. Both men and women in the trade flourish in a network of lunches and drinks dates, parties at galleries, club-hopping. A publicity agent in the city once told me there are only five hundred people who really matter in the media businesses of New York, because they are out and about and visible; the thousands of others who toil in offices inhabit a kind of Siberia. The elite network operates by "buzz," that high-voltage current of rumor flowing day and night in the city.

It didn't seem a good milieu for Rose to spread her wings. On the other hand, you can reach the point when it seems as though if you don't do something new then your life, like a well-worn suit, will become ever shabbier. Rose seized her opportunity with the wisdom of a small business owner; she leased rather than sold the Trout in case things didn't pan out.

The Trout, in the view of all regulars, suffered a subtle but profound decline when Rose left. The new manager was relentlessly friendly. She filled the windows with houseplants; salsa and other healthy snacks replaced the greasy peanuts long favored by the clientele. She possessed that combination of human indifference and bodily cleanliness I associate with Californian culture.

After only a year, though, Rose was back. The unobstructed sight of walking feet almost immediately replaced the houseplants, the greasy nuts returned. For a week the woman from California hung on, and then she too disappeared. We were immensely relieved, of course, but we wondered. At first Rose would only explain that "you can't make any real money in a corporation," a statement apparently logical to the unemployed actors. To me Rose was uncharacteristically evasive. Every once in a while during the first few weeks she'd let slip a bitter comment about "slick uptown kids." Finally, she said, apropos of nothing, "I lost my nerve."

The simplest reason I supposed Rose returned early was culture shock. In stark contrast to the daily reckonings of success and failure, profit and loss, she used in running a small business, the advertising firm operated mysteriously—though in this business the puzzles have to do with human success and failure rather than the operation of machines. One day back at the Trout, she remarked to me an "odd thing" about the people who make it in the image business. The successful people in advertising are not necessarily the most ambitious, since everyone is driven. The really successful ones seem the most adept at walking away from disaster, leaving others to hold the bag; success consists in avoiding the reckonings of the accountant's bottom line. "The trick is, let nothing stick to you." To be sure, there is in every enterprise in the end a bottom line. What struck Rose was that even after such a reckoning, a person's past record of failures counted for less to employers than contacts and networking skills.

That discounting of actual performance applied to her as well. Though she had a formal two-year contract, "they made clear that they could buy me out and let me go at any time." Since she had leased the bar, this didn't prove a mortal threat. What got under her skin was more subtle: she felt constantly on trial, yet she never knew exactly where she stood. There were no objective measures which applied to doing a good job, apart from buzzing and whatever skill is required to "let nothing stick to you." And this was particularly disturbing because Rose was making a personal experiment. She hadn't entered this world to make it big financially, only to do something more interesting with her life. Yet after a year, she told me, "I didn't feel I was getting anywhere; I just didn't know."

In fluid situations like this, people tend to focus on the minutiae of daily events, seeking in details some portent of meaning—rather like ancient priests studying the entrails of slaughtered animals. How the boss says hello in the morning, who got invited just to drinks at the lemon vodka launch and who got invited to the dinner after: these are the portents of what is really happening in the office. Rose could deal practically with anxiety of this trivial, daily sort; she was one of the most sturdy human beings I've known. But the feeling that she had no anchor in the glittery seas of the image business wore her down inside.

Moreover, in the advertising agency she learned a bitter truth about the past experience she brought to her gamble on a different life: middle-aged people like her are treated like deadwood, their accumulated experience taken to be of little value. Everything in the office focused on the immediate moment, on what was just about to break, on getting ahead of the curve; eyes glaze over in the image business when someone begins a sentence "One thing I've learned is that . . ."

It takes courage for a middle-aged person like Rose to risk something new, but uncertainty about where she stood combined with the denial of her lived experience sapped her nerve. "Change," "opportunity," "new": all rang hollow by the time she decided to return to the Trout. Though her willingness to risk was unusual, though the media business is unusually fluid and superficial, her failure illustrates some more general confusions about orienting oneself in a flexible world.

RISK TAKING CAN BE in many different circumstances a highly charged test of character. In nineteenth-century novels, figures like Stendhal's Julien Sorel or Balzac's Vautrin develop themselves psychologically through taking big chances, and in their willingness to risk everything they become nearly heroic figures. When the economist Joseph Schumpeter invokes the creative destruction practiced by the entrepreneur, he writes in the spirit of those novelists: exceptional human beings develop by living constantly on the edge. The traits of character evinced at Davos, letting go of the past and dwelling in disorder, are also ways of living on the edge.

The willingness to risk, however, is no longer meant to be the province only of venture capitalists or extraordinarily adventurous individuals. Risk is to become a daily necessity shouldered by the masses. The sociologist Ulrich Beck declares that in "advance modernity the social production of wealth is systematically accompanied by the social productions of risks."[55] In a more homely vein, the authors of *Upsizing the Individual in the Downsized Corporation* invoke the image of work being continually repotted, like a growing plant, with the worker as the gardener. The very instability of flexible organizations forces upon workers the need to "repot," i.e., take risks with, their work. This business manual is typical of many others in making a virtue out of that necessity. The theory is that you rejuvenate your energies by taking risks, and recharge continually.[56] That "repotting" image is comforting; it domesticates the heroism of risk. Instead of the life-shaking drama of Lucien Sorel's gambles, risk becomes normal and ordinary.

The word "risk" itself descends from the Renaissance Italian word for "to dare," *risicare.* The root does indeed suggest an attitude of bravado and confidence, but this is not the whole story. Up to relatively recently, games of chance and risk-taking appeared to dare the gods. The modern phrase "tempting fate" comes from Greek tragedy, in which Ate, the force of fate, punishes men and women for the pride of daring too much, of presuming on the future. Fortuna, the Roman goddess of chance, was believed to determine every throw of the dice. In this universe governed by gods or God, there was room for daring but not much scope for chance.

A famous book on risk, Fibonacci's *Liber Abaci,* marked a milestone in asserting both the purely random character of events and the capacity of human beings to manage their risks. Fibonacci's book appeared in 1202, and drew on the practice of Arabic mathematicians in writing in numbers like 1, 2, or 804738, which permitted calculations of a sort which could not easily be made with the old Roman numerals I, II, or MCIV. Fibonacci's "rabbits" formed the most celebrated part of the book; he sought to predict how many rabbits would be born in a year from a single pair of parents. From such calculations came a whole mathematical science of predicting outcomes. Renaissance Italian mathematicians like Paccioli and Cardano took up the new science of calculating risk, as did Pascal and Fermat in France. Many of the calculative strategies used in modern computers derive in turn from the work of Jacob Bernoulli and his nephew Daniel Bernoulli at the dawn of the Enlightenment.

As late as the mid-1700s, people tried to understand risk simply through verbal discussion; the insurance company Lloyd's of London, for instance, began as a coffeehouse in which strangers chatted and exchanged information about shipping and other risky ventures, some of these talkers making investment decisions based on what they heard.[57] The revolution launched by Fibonacci eventually replaced discussion with impersonal calculation, as in the projections which make possible the elaborate side bets, derivatives, and hedges of the modern financial machine.

Still, the fear of tempting fate has hung over the management of risk. "Who can pretend to have penetrated so deeply into the nature of the human mind or the wonderful structure of the body [on which] games depend," Jacob Bernoulli asked in 1710, "that he would venture to predict when this or that player would win or lose?"[58] Purely mathematical reckoning cannot displace the psychological aspects of analyzing risks; in his *Treatise on Probability* John Maynard Keynes declared that "there is little likelihood of our discovering a method of recognizing particular probabilities, without any assistance whatever from intuition or direct judgment."[59] What people focus on emotionally, the psychologist Amos Tversky has argued, is loss.

As a result of numerous laboratory experiments, Tversky came to the conclusion that in everyday life people are more concerned about losses than gains when they take risks in their careers or marriages as well as at the gaming table, that "people are much more sensitive to negative than to positive stimuli. . . . There are a few things that would make you feel better, but the numbers of things that would make you feel worse is unbounded."[60] Tversky and his colleague Daniel Kahneman have tried to uncover in particular what might be called a mathematics of fear. Their work is based on the phenomenon of regression, the fact that any one successful bet on the roll of the dice does not lead to a further successful bet, but rather regresses to an indeterminate mean; the next roll could be good or bad.[61] The immediate moment is ruled by blind chance, not by God.

It's for these reasons that risk-taking is something other than a sunny reckoning of the possibilities contained in the present. The mathematics of risk offer no assurances, and the psychology of risk-taking focuses quite reasonably on what might be lost.

This is how Rose's life gambling proceeded. "I was high the first few weeks; no more Manolo, even, Richard sweetie, no more you. I was a corporation executive. Then of course I did begin to miss you all, just a bit, and of course I hated what that blond sun-bunny was doing to my business." Rose paused on this. "But what really got to me . . . it wasn't really so specific." Of course, I said, any person our age is bound to feel apprehensive; the place sounded chaotic and irrational. "No, not even that. I was depressed just by the sheer fact of doing something new." The research of Tversky and Kahnmann suggests that in talking about risk, we use the locution "being at risk"; being at risk is inherently more depressing than promising. Dwelling in a continual state of vulnerability is the proposal which, perhaps unwittingly, the authors of business manuals make when celebrating daily risk-taking in the flexible corporation. To be sure, in Rose's case she was not clinically depressed; she seems to have done her work energetically. Rather, she knew a kind of dull, continual worry, reinforced by the exaggerated ambiguity of success and failure in the advertising business.

Inherent in all risk is regression to the mean. Each particular role of the dice is random. Put another way, risk-taking lacks mathematically the quality of a narrative, in which one event leads to and conditions the next. People can of course deny the fact of regression. The gambler does so when saying he or she is in luck, is on a winning streak, is hot; the gambler talks as though the rolls of the dice are somehow connected, and the act of risking thereby takes on the qualities of a narrative.

But this is a dangerous story. In the evocative formulation of Peter Bernstein, "we pay excessive attention to low-probability events accompanied by high drama and overlook events that happen in routine fashion. . . . as a result, we forget about regression to the mean, overstay our positions, and end up in trouble."[62] Dostoevsky's *The Gambler* could have served Bernstein, Tversky, and Kahneman as an example of how desire for a dramatic narrative of risk is deflated by knowledge of the fictitious character of luck. In the novel, as in life, the need for things to work out combines with the gambler's knowledge that there is no necessity they should.

I asked Rose a more focused version of the question about life narrative I'd asked Rico: what is the story you'd tell about that year uptown? "Story?" How did things change over the course of the year? "Well, in that way they didn't; I was always back at square one." But that can't be true; they kept you even though they let four other new people go. "Yeah, I survived." So they must have liked your work. "Look, these gentlemen have very short memories. Like I said, you're always starting over, you have to prove yourself every day." Being continually exposed to risk can thus eat away at your sense of character. There is no narrative which can overcome regression to the mean, you are always "always starting over."

THIS ELEMENTAL STORY, however, might have a different coloring in a different society. The sociological dimension of Rose's exposure to risk lies in how institutions shape an individual's efforts to change his or her life. We have seen some of the reasons that modern institutions are not themselves rigid and clearly defined; their uncertain character arises through taking aim at routine, through emphasizing short-term activities, through creating amorphous, highly complex networks in place of military-style bureaucracies. Rose's risk-taking occurred in a society seeking to deregulate both time and space.

Risk is a matter of moving from one position to another. One of the most powerful analyses of movement in modern society has come from the sociologist Ronald Burt. The title of one of his books, *Structural Holes,* suggests the peculiarity of changing places in a loose organization; the more gaps, detours, or intermediaries between people in a network, the easier it is for individuals to move around. Uncertainty in the network abets the chances for movement; an individual can take advantage of opportunities not foreseen by others, can exploit weak controls by central authority. The "holes" in an organization are the sites of opportunity, not the clearly defined slots for promotion in a traditional bureaucratic pyramid.

Of course, sheer chaos cannot alone be the risk-taker's friend. The sociologist James Coleman notes that people must draw upon a fund of social capital—shared past experiences as well as individual achievements and endowments—to help navigate a loose network. Other sociologists of network mobility emphasize that a person who presents himself or herself to a new employer or work group has to be attractive as well as available; risk involves more than simply opportunity.[63]

Burt's work points to an important human fact also conveyed concretely by the court at Davos: the good risk-taker has to dwell in ambiguity and uncertainty. The men of Davos have proved themselves at home in this condition. Less powerful individuals who try to exploit ambiguity wind up feeling exiles. Or, in moving, they lose their way. In flexible capitalism, the disorientation entailed in moving toward uncertainty, toward those structural holes, occurs in three specific ways: through "ambiguously lateral moves," "retrospective losses," and unpredictable wage outcomes.

As pyramidal hierarchies are replaced by looser networks, people who change jobs experience more often what sociologists have called "ambiguously lateral moves." These are moves in which a person in fact moves sideways even while believing he or she is moving up in the loose network. This crablike motion occurs, the sociologist Manuel Castells argues, even though incomes are becoming more polarized and unequal; job categories are becoming more amorphous.[64] Other students of social mobility emphasize what are called "retrospective losses" in a flexible network. Since people who risk making moves in flexible organizations often have little hard information about what a new position will entail, they realize only in retrospect they've made bad decisions. They wouldn't have taken the risk if only they'd known. But organizations are so often in a state of internal flux that it's useless to attempt rational decision-making about one's future based on the current structure of one's company.[65]

The most hardheaded calculation people want to make in moving is whether they will earn more money; the statistics on the wages of change in the current economy are discouraging.

Today more people lose than gain through making company job changes; 34 percent significantly lose, 28 percent significantly gain. (Please see Table 8.) A generation ago the numbers were roughly reversed; you did slightly better by moving to a new company than through promotion within. Even so, the rate of intercompany job change was lower then than today; factors like job security and company commitment held people in place.

Tracing the statistical pathways which establish these patterns, I want to emphasize, requires a complex foray into a thicket of age, parents' class background, race, education, and sheer luck. Matters are hardly made clear by making finer distinctions. It appears, for instance, that stockbrokers who have been fired "for poor performance" are twice as likely to gain by changing as stockbrokers who say they have left a firm voluntarily. Why this should be is not self-evident. Few people can do their own research.

For all three reasons, occupational mobility in contemporary societies is often an illegible process. It contrasts, for instance, to negotiations between unions representing massive blocks of workers and managers controlling equally large institutions. These made clear collective gains and losses of income, as well as determining promotion or demotion; such dealings between labor and management were entirely categorical. In the apt phrase of the business analyst Rosabeth Moss Kantor, now the old bureaucratic "elephants are learning to dance."[66] Part of that new dance is to resist categorical negotiations in large institutions, and instead to plot more fluid and individualized paths for promotion or salaries. At General Motors, wage scales and job definitions are infinitely more complicated today than in the middle of the century when Daniel Bell found a rigid, collective regime to rule.

If people don't know what's going to happen when they take the risk of moving, why gamble? The Boston bakery is an interesting case in this regard because the firm has never had to downsize its operations; on the contrary, it is constantly looking for workers. People are not forced out; instead its employees leave voluntarily, as in fact did the man who declared to me, "I won't be doing this the rest of my life." The top managers are defensive about these departures; they point to how safe, attractive, and up-to-date the workplace is. Rodney Everts is less defensive but equally perplexed. "When somebody tells me there's no future here, I ask what they want. They don't know; they tell me you shouldn't be stuck in one place." Fortunately, the job market in Boston for low-wage workers is strong at the moment, but there is something puzzling about the sheer impulse to get out.

When I told Everts about the sociological writing on structural holes, he responded, "Thus science shows us human beings are drawn to danger, like the moth to the flame." (As I say, he is an attentive reader of King James prose.) Yet the impulse to risk-taking, blind, uncertain, or dangerous as it may be, speaks to a more cultural set of motivations.

If all risk-taking is a journey into the unknown, the voyager usually has in mind some destination. Odysseus wanted to find his way home; Julien Sorel wanted to find his way into the upper classes. The modern culture of risk is peculiar in that failure to move is taken as a sign of failure, stability seeming almost a living death. The destination therefore matters less than the act of departure. Immense social and economic forces shape the insistence on departure: the disordering of institutions, the system of flexible production—material realities themselves setting out to sea. To stay put is to be left out.

The decision to depart therefore seems already like a consummation; what matters is that you have decided to make a break. Numerous studies of risk-taking point out that the stimulating "high" comes for people when they first decide to make a break, to depart. This was true for Rose as well. But after this initial exhilaration the tale didn't end. Rose was always starting over, exposed every day. The mathematics of chance, inherently depressing, were compounded for her by a corporate world in which she never knew the stakes on the table. That indeterminacy is true for others seeking more cash or a better position.

For people with weak or superficial attachments to work, like the bakers, there is little reason to remain on shore. Some material markers of the journey would be occupational or wage gains, but lateral moves, retrospective losses, and illegible wage patterns efface these markers of progress. So orienting oneself socially becomes difficult, more difficult than in the class system of the past.

It's not that inequality and social distinction have disappeared—anything but. Rather, it's as though by setting oneself in motion one suddenly suspends one's reality; one is not so much calculating, rationally choosing, but simply hoping that by making a break something will turn up. Much of the literature on risk discusses strategy and game plans, costs and benefits, in a kind of academic dreaming. Risk in real life is driven more elementally by the fear of failing to act. In a dynamic society, passive people wither.

IT MIGHT SEEM, therefore, that risk-taking would be less dispiriting if it were indeed possible to realize the academic strategist's dream, to calculate gains and losses rationally, make risk legible. But modern capitalism has organized certain kinds of risk in a fashion which makes that clarity no more inspiring. New market conditions oblige large numbers of people to take quite demanding risks even though the gamblers know the possibilities of reward are slight.

To illustrate this, I'd like to elaborate on a chance remark Rose made to me one afternoon about what happened each time one of the black suits was fired at the advertising agency. "We had people lined up outside the halls, hundreds of résumés, kids begging us just for a chance to be interviewed." The problem is all too familiar; there are large oversupplies of qualified young workers in many other pursuits, like architecture, academia, and the law.

There are, to be sure, solid material reasons to get a degree. American data (which are representative of all advanced economies) show that increases in income in the last decade were about 34 percent more for workers with a college degree than workers with a high school diploma—that is, the college-educated, who started out earning more, increased the disparity between themselves and their less-educated peers by 34 percent in a single decade. Most Western societies have opened the doors of the institutions of higher education; it is estimated that by 2010, of people aged twenty-five, 41 percent of those in the United States will have a four-year college degree, 62 percent at least a two-year college degree; the rates for Britain and Western Europe are predicted to be about 10 percent lower.[67] Yet only a fifth of jobs in the American labor force in America require a college degree, and the percentage of these highly qualified jobs is only slowly rising. (Please see Table 9.)

Overqualification is a sign of the polarization which marks the new regime. The economist Paul Krugman explains growing inequality in terms of the value of technical skill: "We raise the wage of skilled people who produce planes [and other high-tech products]," he writes, "and lower the wage of those who are unskilled."[68] A leading investment banker and diplomat concurs; Felix Rohatyn believes that an immense shift is occurring in society, "a huge transfer of wealth from lower-skilled, middle-class American workers to the owners of capital assets and to a new technological aristocracy."[69] Such a technological elite, the sociologist Michael Young foresaw fifty years ago in his essay *Meritocracy,* is defined and certified by formal education.[70]

Under these conditions, a kind of extreme risk-taking takes form in which large numbers of young people gamble that they will be one of the chosen few. Such risk-taking occurs in what the economists Robert Frank and Philip Cook call "winner-take-all markets." In this competitive landscape, those who succeed sweep the board of gains, while the mass of losers have crumbs to divide up among themselves. Flexibility is a key element in allowing such a market to form. Without a bureaucratic system to channel wealth gains throughout a hierarchy, rewards gravitate to the most powerful; in an unfettered institution, those in a position to grab everything do so. Flexibility thus accentuates inequality via the winner-take-all market.[71]

In the view of these economists, the "pay-off structure [of the modern economy] has led too many [individuals] to abandon productive alternatives in pursuit of the top prizes."[72] Of course, this is good parental advice: be realistic. But this advice is tinged with a belief which can be traced back to Adam Smith, that such risks are taken in a spirit of unrealistic self-estimation. In *The Wealth of Nations* Smith wrote of the "overweening conceit which the greater part of men have of their abilities. . . . the chance of gain is by every man more or less overvalued, and the chance of loss is by most men undervalued."[73] Frank and Cook report in this regard a recent study of a million American high school seniors in which 70 percent thought they had above-average leadership ability and 2 percent thought they were below average.

But "overweening conceit" seems to me a misreading of the relation between risk and character. Not to gamble is to accept oneself in advance as a failure. Most people who enter winner-take-all markets know the likelihood of failure, but they suspend that knowledge. As with the risk-taking which occurs under less determined conditions, the immediate excitement about striking out may help blot out rational knowledge about the likelihood of success. But even if someone entering a winner-take-all market remains clear-sighted throughout, to do nothing seems passive rather than prudent.

That attitude can be traced back, as an idea, to the early celebrations of the trader in the political economics of Smith and Mill. The imperative to take risks is more widely distributed in modern culture. Risk is a test of character: the important thing is to make the effort, take the chance, even if you know *rationally* you are doomed to fail. That attitude is reinforced by a common psychological phenomenon.

Confronted by something conflicted, a person's attention can become riveted on its immediate circumstances rather than on a long view. Social psychology names attentiveness bred in this way "cognitive dissonance"—conflicting frames of meaning. (Work on cognitive dissonance has been done variously by Gregory Bateson, Lionel Festinger, and myself.)[74] Rose's need for some proof that she was doing a good job even though the corporation on Park Avenue didn't furnish such proof is a classic form of cognitive dissonance. Engagement with such conflicts arouses "focal attention"—which means simply that a person marks a problem as in need of focused attention right now.

When a person lacks belief that anything can be done to solve the problem, long-term thinking can be suspended as useless. However, focal attention may remain active. In this state, people will turn over and over again the immediate circumstances in which they are caught, aware that something needs to be done even though they do nothing. Suspended focal attention is a traumatic reaction found in all higher animals; the rabbit's eyes dwell on the fox's paws.

For a human being, the aftermath of an act of risk can lead to suspended focal attention of the same sort. "Never getting anywhere," "always at square one," confronted by seemingly meaningless success or the impossibility of reward for effort: in all these emotional states, time seems to grind to a halt; the person in these toils becomes prisoner of the present, fixated on its dilemmas. This immobilizing trauma held Rose in its grip for several months until she recovered from her risk uptown and returned to the Trout.

ROSE'S STATEMENT "I lost my nerve" points to a more brutal and less complicated way people can feel at risk. It comes just from living into middle age. The current conditions of corporate life are full of prejudices against middle age, disposed to deny the worth of a person's past experience. Corporate culture treats the middle-aged as risk-averse, in the gambler's sense. But these prejudices are hard to combat. In the high-pressure, shifting world of the modern corporation the middle-aged can easily come to fear that they are eroding from within.

For Rose, the initial shock she received moving uptown to the Park Avenue office hive was that she suddenly became aware just how old she was—not only biologically but socially. "I looked around at these professional girls—and they were girls; they look good, they've got those Locust Valley lock-jaws"—an upper-class New York accent. Rose could never efface her nasal, lower-middle-class speech, but she tried to alter her appearance to look younger. "I paid a woman at Bloomingdale's to buy me better clothes; I got soft contacts, which were horrible," for some reason irritating her eyes; at the office she looked like a woman constantly on the verge of tears. The prejudices against her age were expressed to Rose in ways not necessarily meant to wound. "When I got the contact lenses the girls in the office goo-goo-ed at me, 'Oh, you look so good.' I didn't know whether to believe them or not."

Perhaps more important, her accumulated experience about how people drink and behave in bars counted for little. At one meeting, a moment came when "they were talking 'lite' this and 'lite' that, and I said, 'Nobody goes to a bar to lose weight.'" How did the others take that? "Like I was an exhibit in a museum: the Old Bar Maid." Rose's barbed communications skills, it should be said, were not those taught in a business school. But she never ceased to feel the sting of age, especially when it came in the form of sympathy from younger fellow workers who felt that she was out of it; like the bosses of the firm, they acted on their prejudices by not inviting her to the clubs and after-hours bars where most of the real work of advertising occurs. Rose was genuinely perplexed that she had been taken on for her practical knowledge, but then disregarded as someone who was too old, past it, over the hill.

One statistical foundation for attitudes toward age in the modern workplace appears in the shortening time framework in which people are employed. The number of men aged fifty-five to sixty-four at work in the United States has dropped from nearly 80 percent in 1970 to 65 percent in 1990. The figures for the United Kingdom are virtually the same; in France the numbers of men at work in late middle age has dropped from nearly 75 percent to just over 40 percent, in Germany from nearly 80 percent to just over 50 percent.[75] There is a

slighter abridgment at the beginning of a working life, the age
young people enter the labor force delayed a few years because of increased emphasis on education. In America and
Western Europe, the sociologist Manuel Castells thus predicts
that "the actual working lifetime could be shortened to about
30 years (from 24 to 54), out of a real lifetime span of about
75–80 years."[76] That is, the productive life span is being compressed to less than half the biological life span, with older
workers leaving the scene long before they are physically or
mentally unfit. Many people Rose's age (she was fifty-three
when she moved uptown) are preparing for retirement.

The emphasis on youth is one consequence of the compres-
sion of working life. In the nineteenth century, the preference
for youth was a matter of cheap labor; the "mill girls" of
Lowell, Massachusetts, and "pit boys" of northern England
worked for wages well below those of adults. In today's capitalism that low-wage preference for youth still exists, most notably in factories and sweatshops of the less developed parts
of the world. But other attributes of youth now seem to make
it appealing in higher reaches of labor, and these lie more in
the realm of social prejudice.

A recent issue of the *California Management Review*, for
instance, sought to explain the positives of youth and the neg-
atives of age in flexible organizations. It did so by arguing that
older workers have inflexible mind-sets and are risk-averse, as
well as lacking in the sheer physical energy needed to cope
with the demands of life in the flexible workplace.[77] The image
of organizational "deadwood" expresses these convictions. An
advertising executive told the sociologist Katherine Newman,
"If you're in advertising, you're dead after thirty. Age is a
killer." A Wall Street executive told her, "Employers think that
[if you are over forty] you can't think anymore. Over fifty and
[they think] you're burned out."[78] Flexibility equals youth,
rigidity equals age.

These prejudices serve several purposes. For instance, they
target older workers as a readily available pool of candidates
for dismissal during corporate reengineering. In the Anglo-

American regime, the rate of involuntary dismissal has doubled in the last twenty years for men in their forties and early fifties. The association of age with rigidity also accounts for much of the pressure corporations put today on executives to retire in their late fifties, even though mentally they may be in their prime.

Older, experienced workers tend to be more judgmental of their superiors than workers just starting out. Their accumulated knowledge endows them with what the economist Albert Hirschmann calls powers of "voice," which means older employees are more likely to speak up against what they see as bad decision-making. They will more often do so out of loyalty to the institution than to a particular manager. Many younger workers are more tolerant of taking bad orders. If they become unhappy, they are more likely to quit, rather than fight within, and for, the organization. They are disposed, as Hirschmann puts it, to "exit."[79] In the advertising agency, Rose found that older admen indeed more frequently spoke up against the bosses, who were often their juniors in age, than did the younger employees. One of these long-serving members of the firm was in turn taunted by his boss, "You may not like it here, but you are too old to get a job anywhere else."

For older workers, the prejudices against age send a powerful message: as a person's experience accumulates, it loses value. What an older worker has learned over the course of the years about a particular company or profession may get in the way of new changes dictated by superiors. From the institution's vantage point, the flexibility of the young makes them more malleable in terms of both risk-taking and immediate submission. Yet this powerful message has a more personal meaning to workers apart from the prejudices of power.

It was Rico who made me aware of this, when he talked about the erosion of his engineering skills. At one point on the airplane, I remarked to Rico that I feel I have to start from scratch each time I write; I gain no greater confidence no matter how many books I publish. Young, solid, full of energy, he responded sympathetically that he often felt "past it" as an engineer. He worried that his skills were eroding from within; though he was twenty years younger than Rose, he said that as an engineer, he was now "just an observer."

This at first seemed patent nonsense. What Rico told me in explanation is that the science knowledge he gained in school is no longer cutting-edge; he understands what's happening in the burgeoning field of information technology, yet says he can no longer stay one step ahead of the field. Younger engineers in their early twenties treat him, now in his late thirties, as somewhat faded. I asked Rico if he'd thought to go back to university for "retraining," at which he eyed me sourly. "We're not talking about learning to press a new set of buttons. I'm too old to start over."

According to Rico, complex skills like his are no longer additive, permitting one to build ever higher on the same foundation; the development of new fields requires a fresh approach from the start, an approach most effectively taken by fresh faces.

An American or European engineer who loses a job to a peer in India working for lower wages has had the practice of skills taken away—which is one version of what sociologists call "deskilling." No one has taken away Rico's engineering knowledge. Rico's fear addresses a weakness he feels occurring within him because of the sheer passage of time. Often, he said, he feels angry when he reads technical journals; "I come across things, and I say to myself, 'I should have thought of that.' But I didn't." Again, he hardly conforms to the stereotype of "deadwood," but about his technical competence he believes equally firmly that he is "over the hill." In this way, the emphasis on youth and his individual interpretation of aging combine. Social prejudice reinforces the internal fear of losing potency.

Rico sees the two sides combine in his office. He employs three young hotshot engineers, ten years younger than he, in his consulting firm. "My main problem is holding on to them." Indeed, he is certain that those whose engineering is more state-of-the-art will abandon him—"The ones who can leave,

leave as soon as they can." Light in loyalty, the young hotshots
are disposed to exit even though Rico is willing to give them
real voice in the company. He feels he can do little about it. "I
have no authority over them, you know?" His experience does
not command their respect.

In her own more modest corner, Rose's time on Park Avenue
gave her a sense that her knowledge was eroding from within.
To her everlasting credit (in my view), Rose had never mixed,
much less heard of, such exotic new cocktails as a Highland
Landmine (one part single-malt scotch and two parts vodka
over shaved ice). But it bothered her not to know, especially
as she covered up by faking at a meeting a long disquisition on
such youth potions. She would, of course, have done better to
tell the truth, but she was afraid doing so would be yet one
more sign she was past it. I doubt Rico is as used up as he
thinks; I know that Rose was not, since she survived while
younger employees were sacked. But for both, when they are
tested, they fear past experience doesn't count.

The new order does not consider that the sheer passage of
time necessary to accumulate skill gives a person standing and
rights—value in a material sense; it views such claims based
on the passage of time to represent yet another face of the evil
of the old bureaucratic system, in which seniority rights froze
institutions. The regime focuses on immediate capability.

Flexible corporate practice, as well as current government
labor policy in Britain and the United States, is based on the
assumption that rapid change of skills is the norm. In fact, his-
torically, the discarding of people with "old" skills usually has
occurred slowly. Two generations were required to displace a
craft skill like weaving in the late eighteenth century, for instance, and the changes at Ford's Highland Park plant required
nearly thirty years at the beginning of the twentieth century.
Perhaps surprisingly, in many manufacturing and office pursuits
today the pace of technological change is still relatively leisure-
ly; as many industrial sociologists have observed, it takes institutions a long time to digest the technologies they ingest.[80] The

passage of time is also necessary to develop new skills; someone who has simply read a carpentry book is not a carpenter.

The time frame of risk offers little personal comfort, despite these long-term historical trends. Indeed, personal anxiety about time is deeply intertwined with the new capitalism. A writer for the *New York Times* recently declared that "job apprehension has intruded everywhere, diluting self-worth, splintering families, fragmenting communities, altering the chemistry of workplaces."[81] Many economists treated this as rubbish; the facts of job creation in the neoliberal order seemed to render it transparently false. Yet the author wrote precisely when he used the word "apprehension." An apprehension is an anxiety about what might happen; apprehension is created in a climate emphasizing constant risk, and apprehension increases when past experience seems no guide to the present.

If the denial of experience were simply an imposed prejudice, we the middle-aged would be simply the victims of institutional youth cult. But the apprehension about time is more deeply etched into us. The passage of years seems to hollow us out. Our experience seems a shameful citation. Such convictions put our sense of self-worth at risk, through the inexorable passage of years rather than by deciding to gamble.

BACK AT THE TROUT, Rose recovered her nerve; she was again in control, until she died of lung cancer. "I suppose it was a mistake," she remarked once about her time uptown as we lingered over cigarettes and drinks, "but I had to do it."

SIX

The Work Ethic

All art," Oscar Wilde declared in the preface to *The Picture of Dorian Gray*, "is at once surface and symbol. Those who go beneath the surface do so at their own peril." [82] The superficialities of modern society are more demeaning than the surfaces and masks of art. Rico's neighbors didn't go much beneath the surface with him. The bakers operate simple user-friendly machines which give them a superficial understanding of their work. Rose went to work at a Park Avenue corporation where the emphasis on youth and good looks—the most fleeting, alas, of human qualities—meant her accumulated experience of life had little value.

One reason for this demeaning superficiality is the disorganization of time. Time's arrow is broken; it has no trajectory in a continually reengineered, routine-hating, short-term political economy. People feel the lack of sustained human relations and durable purposes. The people I've so far described have all tried to find the depth of time beneath the surface, if only by registering unease and anxiety about the present.

The work ethic is the arena in which the depth of experience is most challenged today. The work ethic, as we commonly understand it, asserts self-disciplined use of one's time and the value of delayed gratification. This discipline of time shaped Enrico's life as it did those of the autoworkers at Willow Run and the Greek bakers in Boston. They worked hard and they waited; this was their psychological experience of depth. Such a work ethic depends in part on institutions stable enough for a person to practice delay. Delayed gratification loses its value, though, in a regime whose institutions change rapidly; it becomes absurd to work long and hard for an employer who thinks only about selling up and moving on.

It would be a morose sentimentalism which merely regretted the decline of hard work and of self-discipline—not to mention good grooming and respect of one's elders and all the other joys of the good old time. The serious business of the old work ethic put heavy burdens on the working self. People sought to prove their own worth through their work; in the form of "worldly asceticism," as Max Weber called it, delayed gratification could become a deeply self-destructive practice. But the modern alternative to the long discipline of time is no real remedy to this self-denial.

The modern work ethic focuses on teamwork. It celebrates sensitivity to others; it requires such "soft skills" as being a good listener and being cooperative; most of all, teamwork emphasizes team adaptability to circumstances. Teamwork is the work ethic which suits a flexible political economy. For all the psychological heavy breathing which modern management does about office and factory teamwork, it is an ethos of work which remains on the surface of experience. Teamwork is the group practice of demeaning superficiality.

THE OLD WORK ETHIC revealed concepts of character which still matter, even if these qualities no longer find expression in labor. The old work ethic was founded on self-disciplined use of one's time, with the emphasis laid on a self-imposed, voluntary practice rather than merely passive submission to schedules or routine. In the ancient world this self-imposed discipline was thought to be the only way to cope with the chaos of nature. It was a necessity required every day of farmers. Here is the advice Hesiod gives them in *Works and Days*:

> Do not postpone for tomorrow or the day after tomorrow; barns are not filled by those who postpone and waste time in aimless-

ness. Work prospers with care; he who postpones wrestles with
ruin.[83]

Nature is uncertain, indifferent; the farmer's world is harsh.
"Men never rest from toil and sorrow by day," Hesiod declared,
"and from perishing by night."[84]

In Hesiod's world, however, self-imposed discipline in using
one's time seemed more brute necessity than human virtue.
Most of the farmers of Hesiod's day were slaves rather than
free yeomen; whether slave or free, the farmer's struggle with
nature seemed of less account than the military battles of city
men with each other. Thucydides later noted with a certain indifference how both Spartans and Athenians laid waste the
countryside of their enemies, as though the farmer's labors
had no moral claim to be spared.

In the course of time, the moral stature of the farmer is ele-
vated. The necessity of hard work becomes a virtue. Virgil,
nearly five hundred years after Hesiod, still invokes the anarchy of Nature, as in the first *Georgics*:

> Often I have seen the raging winds
> Tear a heavy crop up by the roots,
> And toss it far and wide, just as the farmer
> Brought in his mowers to strip the barley:
> The storm in a black and twisting cloud,
> Swept away both the blade and the writhing grain.[85]

Virgil, like Hesiod, understands the most a farmer can do in
the face of this whirlwind is try to husband his use of time. But
thanks to the very determination of the farmer to endure, he
has become a hero of sorts.

Here lies the sense of the famous passage, in the second
book of the *Georgics,* in which Virgil describes soldiers engaged "in dubious battle"; the farmer stands apart from their
struggles, and from those of the "Roman State, and empires
doomed to die."[86] The farmer knows there are no decisive victories over nature—victory is an illusion. For Virgil, the moral
virtue of farming is that it teaches *permanent* resolution re-
gardless of outcome. And in the *Georgics* Virgil gives Hesiod's

adage "He who postpones wrestles with ruin" a new meaning. The "farmer" in all of us wrestles with the capacity to ruin himself. The *Georgics* transposes the anarchy of nature into a vision of inner, psychic anarchy; against these inner storms the individual's only defense is to organize well his or her time.

As the notion of self-discipline first took form, it thus contained a strong dose of stoicism—not of the philosophical sort, but a kind of practical stoicism which dictated the permanent need to combat inner anarchy without expectation of victory. Passing into early Christian beliefs, this practical stoicism shaped early church doctrines about sloth—sloth appearing less a state of sybaritic pleasure than an inner decomposition of the self. For nearly a thousand years, from St. Augustine's depiction of sloth in the *Confessions* to the early Renaissance, this practical stoicism held firm its ethical grip. The scheduling of time, as in the ringing of church bells, could assist men and women in organizing their time, but not instill the desire for self-discipline—that desire could be generated only by a deeper apprehension of pervasive chaos within and without.

Something happened in the early Renaissance to this deep-rooted practical stoicism. It was not directly challenged as an ethical value, but was affected nonetheless by a new appreciation of human beings as historical creatures, creatures who do not simply endure year after year but rather evolve and change. The farmer's permanent stoicism would not suffice for historical man; the terms of discipline would have to adapt to a self in flux. But how?

This was the dilemma which faced the Renaissance Florentine philosopher Pico della Mirandola in his *Oration on the Dignity of Man*. Pico is the first modern voice of *homo faber*, that is, "man as his own maker." Pico asserted that "man is an animal of diverse, multiform, and destructible nature."[87] In this pliant condition, "it is given to [man] to have that which he chooses and to be that which he wills."[88] Rather than maintain the world as we inherited it, we have to shape it afresh; our dignity depends on doing so. Pico declares, "It is ignoble . . . to give birth to nothing from ourselves."[89] Our work in the world is to create, and the greatest creation is to shape our own life histories. The virtue of imposing a shape on experience remains a fundamental way to define someone possessed of a strong character.

Homo faber ran up, however, against traditional Christian dogma. St. Augustine warned, "Hands off yourself; try to build up yourself and you build a ruin." A Christian obeying St. Augustine should seek to imitate instead the life and example of Jesus. Thus the Renaissance Bishop Tyndale counseled a parishioner to "feeleth him self . . . altered and fashioned like unto Christ." Any purely personal creation will necessarily be inferior.[90] It is a virtue to discipline the use of one's time, but a sin of pride to design one's own experience.

Pico was not deaf to these convictions. He too believed that Christian conduct requires self-discipline and the imitation of exemplary lives. But against this his imagination of historical time is formed by literary models of the spiritual journey; Pico invokes Odysseus the sailor, whose wanderings create their own self-contained history, even though the sailor never doubts his ultimate goal. The Christian in Pico is certain of the final destination, but Pico also wants to put out to sea. He is one of the first Renaissance philosophers to celebrate psychic risks, knowing that the sea within, like the oceans navigated by Renaissance explorers, is uncharted territory.

These two contrary ethical strands, self-discipline and self-fashioning, came together in the most celebrated essay on the work ethic, Max Weber's *The Protestant Ethic and the Spirit of Capitalism*. He sought to show their combination rather than contradiction in analyzing the dawn of modern capitalism. To be sure, Weber believed that Hesiod's old injunction to the farmer "Do not delay" was partly reversed in capitalism to become "You must delay." What you must delay is your desire for gratification and fulfillment; you have to fashion your life history so that at the end you have achieved something; then, and only then, in that future time, will you be fulfilled. For the present, you must still act like Virgil's farmer, combating sloth and the forces of inner chaos by a rigid, grim apportioning of your time. This work ethic—to be blunt—Weber thought a fraud. Delay is endless, self-denial in the present is relentless; the promised rewards never come.

This view of working time serves Weber as a way to criticize modern beliefs in character, specifically, beliefs in man as his own maker. The version of Weber's essay most often purveyed in school runs something as follows. The seventeenth century Protestant sought to offer proof of his worthiness in the sight of God by disciplining himself, but unlike the Catholic penitent in a monastery, he would show he was worthy through his work, denying himself in the present, accumulating little tokens of virtue through daily sacrifice. This self-denial then became the "worldly asceticism" of eighteenth-century capitalist practice, with its emphasis on saving rather than spending, its "routinization" of everyday activity, its fear of pleasure. Such a neat little package manages to empty Weber's writing of its tragic grandeur.

Christianity, in his view, is a distinctive faith because it plunges men and women into profoundly painful doubt by requiring them to ask themselves, "Am I a worthy human being?" The Fall and its consequences seem to answer that question decisively: I am not. But no religion could assert an unrelieved vision of human unworthiness; it would be a prescription for suicide. Catholicism before the advent of Protestantism had sought to reassure flawed humanity though counseling surrender to the institutions of the church, its rituals, and the magic powers of its priests. Protestantism sought a more individual remedy for doubt of self.

Oddly, Martin Luther should have been Weber's exemplary figure, but isn't. In Luther's "95 Theses" the rebellious pastor opposed to the comforts of ritual a more naked experience of faith; faith could not come, Luther asserted, through smelling incense or praying to statues and paintings. Attacks on icons have had a long history in the church, as in Islam and Judaism. But Luther was distinctive in maintaining that the man or

woman who renounced idolatry had to face questions of faith
unaided and alone, rather than as a member of a community.
His is a theology of the individual.

The Protestant individual had to shape his or her history so
that it would add up to a meaningful, worthy whole. The individual now becomes ethically responsible for his or her own,
particular, lived time; Pico's voyager is to be judged morally by
the narrative of how he or she has lived—down to the details
of how much sleep one has allowed oneself, how one has
trained one's children to talk. We are able to control so little of
what happens in our life history, yet Luther insists that we
must take responsibility for the whole of it.[91]

In *The Protestant Ethic,* Weber zeroed in upon an aspect of
Protestant doctrine which made taking responsibility for one's
life history impossible. Luther had declared that "no one is
sure of the integrity of his own contrition."[92] The Christian
dwells in unrelieved doubt about being able to justify the story
of his or her life. In Protestant theology this unrelieved doubt
is conveyed through the seemingly arcane theological doctrine of predestination. Calvin declares in the *Institutes* that
only God knows whether a soul is to be saved or damned after
death; we cannot presume on divine Providence. Crushed by
the weight of sinfulness, humans beings thus dwell in a state of
permanent insecurity, uncertain whether life will lead to an
eternity of burning torment. This is Protestant humanity's unhappy lot: we must earn our moral standing, yet can never
presume confidently to say "I am good," nor even "I have done
what is good"; all that is possible to say is "I mean well."
Calvin's God replies, "Try harder. Whatever is, is not good
enough."

Again this risks being a prescription for suicide. But the
Protestant was offered in place of ritual's balm a harsher med-
icine: relentless hard work oriented to the future. Organizing
one's life history through hard work might serve as a small
light in the dark, a "sign of election" that one might be among
those saved from hell. Unlike Catholic good works, though,
hard work couldn't earn the Protestant any greater favor with

the Creator; labor merely offers signs of worthy intentions to a divine Judge who has already decided every case in advance.

This is the terror which lurks behind the abstract concept of "worldly asceticism." In Weber's view there passed from Protestant to capitalist the willingness to save rather than to spend as an act of self-discipline and self-denial. This same passage gave birth to a new character type. It is the driven man, bent on proving his moral worth through his work.

Weber invoked an American icon as an early example of the driven man. Benjamin Franklin, the witty and worldly diplomat, inventor, and statesman, appears in Weber's pages as pleasure-fearing and work-obsessed beneath his affable exterior, Franklin reckoning every moment of time as though it were money, constantly denying himself an ale or a pipe in order to save, each penny put aside serving in Franklin's mind as a little token of virtue. As diligently as a man or woman practices the work ethic, though, self-doubt persists. Franklin carries the persistent fear he is not good enough just as he is, yet no accomplishment ever seems enough; there are no consummations in this scheme of things.

The driven man does not conform to the old Catholic images of the vices of wealth, such as gluttony or luxury; the driven man is intensely competitive but cannot enjoy what he gains. The life history of the driven man becomes an endless quest for recognition from others and for self-esteem. Yet even if others would praise him for his worldly asceticism, he would fear accepting that praise, for it would mean accepting himself. Everything in the present is treated as an instrumental means to a final destination; nothing right now matters for its own sake. This is what became in secular society of the theology of the individual.

As economic history, *The Protestant Ethic and the Spirit of Capitalism* is riddled with errors. As economic analysis, it strangely omits any consideration of consumption as a driving force in capitalism. As the critique of a certain character type, however, both its purpose and its execution are coherent. The work ethic of the driven man appears to Max Weber no source of human happiness, nor indeed of psychological strength. The driven man is too heavily weighed down by the importance he has come to attach to work. Discipline, Michel Foucault tells us, is an act of self-punishment, and it certainly appears so in this rendition of the work ethic.[93]

I've gone into this history in some detail because the disciplined use of one's time is not the simple, straightforward virtue it may at first appear. A grim, relentless struggle in the ancient world, a conundrum for Renaissance believers in *homo faber,* a source of self-punishment in the theology of the individual: Surely the weakening of the work ethic would be a gain for civilization. Surely we want to exorcise the furies besetting the driven man.

IT DEPENDS, HOWEVER, on how the weight upon the working self is lightened. Modern forms of teamwork are in many ways the opposites of the work ethic as Max Weber conceived it. An ethic of the group as opposed to the individual, teamwork emphasizes mutual responsiveness rather than personal validation. The time of teams is flexible and oriented to specific, short-term tasks, rather than the reckoning of decades marked by withholding and waiting. Teamwork, though, takes us into that domain of demeaning superficiality which besets the modern workplace. Indeed, teamwork exits the realm of tragedy to enact human relations as a farce.

Take the matter of vodka. During Rose's year on Park Avenue, her advertising firm faced an evidently perennial problem. Since this liquor has no taste, the marketing task is to convince a buyer that one brand is nevertheless superior to any other. Rose, I am sorry to say, put this conundrum to her financial advantage when running the Trout; she filled empty bottles of Stolichnaya vodka from Russia with a cheap vodka made somewhere in Canada. "No one has yet tasted the difference," she once confessed to me with a certain pride.

During her year uptown, one of the liquor companies proposed shoving a mountain of money at this dilemma and ran a competition of sorts among ad agencies for a solution. New bottle shapes, impossible Russian names, new and weird flavors, even the shape of the boxes in which vodka is sold—all were on the table for discussion. In this little comedy, Rose had her own solution, one which I suspect she advanced with a certain irony. She pointed out that there existed Russian vodkas flavored with honey; these could be pushed as health drinks.

What made this comedy serious for Rose was that she soon came to be left out of the loop—that is, out of the communications network of mutual suggestion and rumor about what other firms were doing that animated the vodka team and its team players. Modern communications technology has in some ways speeded up the process of collaboration, but in the media industry, at least in New York, face-to-face still is the major means of transmission. She was not part of this face-to-face "buzz" at parties, clubs, and restaurants outside the office; her age and her looks, as we've seen, were against her.

But more than this, she kept intruding information about how people actually drink in bars, which lay outside the purview of those who were in the loop. For instance, she mentioned that vodka is a drink of choice for people who are secret alcoholics, since they believe no one can smell they've been drinking. Her colleagues reacted as if this were her private knowledge, disturbing their own discussions. Specialized information often tends to jam the system of communication. In teamwork of a nonmaterial sort, where people are working together on an image, the act of communication is more important than the facts communicated; to communicate, the playing field of talk needs to be open and accessible. Once that happens, the shaping and sharing of rumor becomes the substance of collaboration. Buzz about competitors provides energy to the communications; hard facts weaken the energies of exchange. Indeed, information exchange tends to be self-exhausting; at the ad agency, the buzz about the Russian-name answer lasted only until it had been fully networked, and then the buzz about hexagonal boxing for the bottles began.

The hardest fact about this group effort was that the agency failed to get the contract. Rose expected that there would ensue a period of mutual recrimination and blame on the team, since the financial consequences for the agency were severe. Moreover, she told me, she expected people to experience "grief" at the loss, by which she meant that these hard-driven ad execs would really care about losing. But as a group, they had a different reaction, more self-protective. There was no mutual recrimination. Nor did people make an effort to justify themselves. There was no time. In a few days, the hard-liquor group had moved on to another project, and moved on as a team.

A specialist in group behavior might well expect this. Groups tend to hold together through keeping to the surface of things; shared superficiality keeps people together by avoiding difficult, divisive, personal questions. Teamwork might seem to be just another example, therefore, of the bonds of group conformity. But the ethos of communication and information-sharing gives conformity a particular twist: the emphasis on being flexible and open to change made members of the team susceptible to the slightest twitches of rumor or suggestion from others on the party-office-lunch-club network. As I have noted, New York adpersons are not corporate conformists of the tight and buttoned-up sort. In the old work culture, the corporate conformist was an all too predictable and reliable character—you knew every response. In this flexible culture of the image and its information, predictability and reliability are less salient character traits; there is no firm footing here, just as there can be no final answer to the problem vodka poses.

Rose's dictum "Let nothing stick to you" applied in this case to the team leader in a particular way. The leader of the hard-liquor team had throughout the vodka campaign acted as an equal to the others rather than as a boss; in management-speak his role was to "facilitate" a solution among the group and to "mediate" between client and team. He is a manager of process. His job, facilitation and mediation, can be, with enough *savoir faire*, divorced from outcome. The word "leader" thus hardly applies to him in the traditional sense of an authority. Nor are facilitation and mediation the grim, resolute acts of will such as formed the characters of the ancient yeomen doing battle with nature.

What I have described may seem hardly worthy of the term "work ethic." And indeed it was a shock to Rose to pass into this corporate milieu. When she worked at the Trout, Rose practiced something like the old-fashioned work ethic. The immediate tasks of getting in supplies and turning out burgers and drinks may have given her little deep satisfaction, but she also worked for the future—to accumulate enough money to put her girls through college and to build up a business worth enough that she could eventually retire on what she could sell it for. Self-denial came naturally to her—until the moment, perhaps mistaken, when she decided she could wait no more, could do something with her life, could set out on Pico's voyage.

Weber's worldly asceticism, as we have seen, realized Luther's theology of the individual in a secular world. The individual caught in the toils of worldly asceticism struggles to gain power over himself or herself. More, the driven man seeks to *justify* himself. In the ad agency, Rose found a different work ethic suited to a firm oriented entirely to the present, its images and its surfaces. In this world, the work ethic took a different form, seemingly more collaborative than individual in its terms, and we might say more forgiving.

Yet it is not quite so benign. People still play games of power in teams, but the emphasis on soft skills of communication, facilitation, and mediation changes radically one aspect of power: authority disappears, authority of the sort which self-confidently proclaims, "This is the right way!" or "Obey me, because I know what I'm talking about!" The person with power does not justify command; the powerful only "facilitate," enable others. Such power without authority disorients employees; they may still feel driven to justify themselves, but now there is no one higher up who responds. Calvin's God has fled. This disappearance of authority figures from teamwork occurs in quite specific and tangible ways.

TEAMWORK ACQUIRED a kind of official sanction in modern American management practice in a study commissioned by Secretary of Labor Elizabeth Dole. The Secretary's Commission on Achieving Necessary Skills (SCANS) produced its report in 1991. It set out to be a report on the skills people need in a flexible economy. As one would expect, the report does make much of basic verbal and math skills, as well as the ability to deal with technology. The surprising thing is that Dole and her colleagues, not known for dewy-eyed sentimentality, put so much emphasis on listening well, on teaching others, and on the art of facilitation in teams.[94]

The SCANS image of the team is of a group of people assembled to perform a specific, immediate task, rather than to dwell together as in a village. The authors reason that a worker has to bring to short-term tasks an instant ability to work well with a shifting cast of characters. That means the social skills people bring to work are *portable*: you listen well and help others, as you move from team to team, as the personnel of teams shifts—as though moving from window to window on a computer screen. Detachment is also required of the good team player: you should have the ability to stand back from established relationships and judge how they can be changed; you must picture the task at hand, rather than be plunged into long histories of intrigue, past betrayals, and jealousies.

The realities of teamwork in the flexible workplace are signaled by the misleading sports metaphor which suffuses this report: in flexible forms of work, the players make up the rules as they go along. The SCANS study emphasizes the art of listening, for instance, because the authors consider talking things through more improvisatory and free than working according to written rules in a manual of procedures. And office sports differ from other sports because the players at work don't keep score in the same way. Only the current game matters. The SCANS study emphasizes that past performance is no guide to present rewards; in each office "game" you start over from the beginning. This is one way to convey that seniority counts for less and less in the modern workplace.

The authors of the SCANS and similar studies are realists: they know the economy today emphasizes immediate performance and short-term, bottom-line results. Yet modern managers also know that individual dog-eat-dog competition can wreck the performance of a group. Thus a fiction arises in modern teamwork at work: employees aren't really competing against each other. And even more important, the fiction arises that workers and bosses aren't antagonists; the boss instead manages group process. He or she is a "leader," the most cunning word in the modern management lexicon; a leader is on your side, rather than your ruler. The game of power is being played by the team against teams in other companies.

Here's how the anthropologist Charles Darrah found workers inducted into this fiction in the "human skills" training of two high-tech manufacturing companies. His research abounds in the delicious ironies which reality brings to theory; for instance, Vietnamese workers who composed about 40 percent of the workforce in one company "were especially fearful of the team concept, which they likened to Communist work teams."[95] Training in such sociable virtues as sharing information proved anything but easy and benign. Higher-status workers feared teaching new or lower-status workers their own skills; they could then be replaced.

Employees learned the portable skills of teamwork through coaching in how to act various company roles, so that every worker would know how to behave in the varied windows of work. In one of Darrah's sites, "workers were advised that each team was to act as a separate company, with the members thinking of themselves as its 'vice presidents.'"[96] Most workers found this somewhat bizarre, since the company was known to treat the Vietnamese factory operatives with scant respect, but the new employees who played along were judged to have "succeeded" in their human-skills training. The time allotted for these sessions was short—a few days, sometimes only a few hours. The shortness mirrors the reality the workers would face in flexible work, requiring quick study of new situations and new people. The audience is, of course, the managers whom the new recruit is trying to impress; the art of feigning in teamwork is to behave as though one were addressing only other employees, as though the boss weren't really watching.

When the sociologist Laurie Graham went to work on the assembly line at a Subaru-Isuzu plant, she found that "the team metaphor was used at all levels of the company," the highest team being the Operating Committee. The sports analogy was out in full force; "team leaders," according to one company document, "are highly skilled Associates, like basketball team captains." The team concept justified flexible labor as a way to develop the individual capacities; the company declared "all Associate members will be trained in—and will perform—a number of functions. This increases their value to the team and to [Subaru-Isuzu]" as well as their own feelings of self-worth.[97] Laurie Graham found herself engulfed in a "culture of cooperation through egalitarian symbols."[98]

The sociologist Gideon Kunda calls such teamwork a kind of "deep acting," because it obliges individuals to manipulate their appearances and behavior with others.[99] "How interesting." "What I heard you saying is . . ." "How could we do this better?" These are the actor's masks of cooperation. The successful players in Darrah's training groups rarely behaved the same way offscreen as they did when the bosses were watching. Indeed, the sociologist Robin Leidner has explored the written scripts which are in fact handed out to employees in service enterprises; what these scripts aim to do is establish the "friendliness" of the employee more than address the substance of a client's concerns. In a turnstile world of work, the masks of cooperativeness are among the only possessions workers will carry with them from task to task, firm to firm— these windows of social skill whose "hypertext" is a winning smile. If this human-skills training is only an act, though, it is a matter of sheer survival. Commenting on people who fail to develop quickly the masks of cooperativeness, one supervisor told Darrah that "most will wind up pumping gas."[100] And within the team, the fictions which deny the individual struggle for power or mutual conflict serve to strengthen the position of those on top.

Laurie Graham found people oppressed in a particular way by the very superficiality of the fictions of teamwork. Peer pressure from other workers on her work team took the place of bosses cracking the whip in order to move the cars as fast as possible along the assembly line; the fiction of cooperating employees served the company's relentless drive for ever greater productivity. After an initial period of enthusiasm, a coworker told her, "I thought this place would be different with its team concept and all, but management is just trying to work people to death." The various work groups were collectively responsible for their members' individual efforts, and teams criticized one another. One worker whom Graham interviewed said a team leader "came up to me and gave me a short lecture on how . . . we work best as a team: 'picking up someone else's mistake and letting them know before it hits the end of the line.'" Workers did hold one another accountable; they were forced to do so in meetings where people engaged in what reads like group therapy—a therapy oriented to the bottom line.[101] But the reward for the individual is reintegration into the group.

The fiction that workers and management are on the same team proved equally useful to Subaru-Isuzu in its dealings with the outside world. Subaru-Isuzu uses this fiction of community at work to help justify its fierce resistance to labor unions; moreover, the fiction of community helps justify the existence of a Japanese company extracting profits in America to be sent home. This company represents an extreme case, in that Japanese firms tend to push teamwork to its limits. But it magnifies a more general deployment of teamwork in flexible institutions. "What these measures have in common," the labor economists Eileen Appelbaum and Rosemary Batt believe, "is that they do not change the fundamental nature of the production system or threaten the basic organization or power structure of the firms."[102]

Most important in this regard is the fact that managers cling to the nostrum of doing the job at hand all together, all on the same team, in order to resist being challenged internally. When Michael Hammer and James Champy urge, in *Reengineering the Corporation,* that managers "stop acting like supervisors and behave more like coaches," they do so for the sake of the boss rather than for the sake of the employee.[103] The boss avoids being held responsible for his or her actions; it's all on the player's shoulders.

To put this more formally, power is present in the superficial scenes of teamwork, but authority is absent. An authority figure is someone who takes responsibility for the power he or she wields. In an old-style work hierarchy, the boss might do that by overtly declaring, "I have the power, I know what's best, obey me." Modern management techniques seek to escape from the "authoritarian" aspect of such declarations, but in the process they manage to escape as well from being held responsible for their acts. "People need to recognize we are all contingent workers in one form or another," says a manager at ATT during a recent spate of downsizing; "We are all victims of time and place."[104] If "change" is the responsible agent, if everybody is a "victim," then authority vanishes, for no one can be held accountable—certainly not this manager letting people go. Instead, peer pressure is meant to do the manager's work.

The repudiation of authority and responsibility in the very superficialities of flexible teamwork structures everyday work life as well as moments of crisis like a strike or a downsizing. Excellent fieldwork on this everyday repudiation of authority by those with power has been done by the sociologist Harley Shaiken, and it is worth quoting at length what one manual worker in a "mixed team" of blue- and white-collar employees told Shaiken about how ducking responsibility occurs:

> Really, what's happening is that you're not running the machine alone—there are three or four people running it—the engineer, the programmer, the guy who made the fixture, the operator. . . . One thing that happens is that it is too hard to communicate

with the other people involved in the process. They don't want to hear it. They've got all the training, all the degrees. They just don't want to hear from you about anything that's gone wrong. It's got to be all your fault. They sure won't admit it if *they've* made a mistake. . . . When I find a way to improve some operation, if I can do it without anyone seeing, I don't tell anyone. For one thing, no one ever asks me.[105]

The Swedish sociologist Malin Åkerström concludes from such experiences that neutrality is a form of betrayal. The absence of real human beings declaring "I'll tell you what to do" or at the extreme "I'll make you suffer" is more than a defensive act within the corporation; this absence of authority frees those in control to shift, adapt, reorganize without having to justify themselves or their acts. In other words, it permits freedom of the moment, a focus just on the present. Change is the responsible agent; change is not a person.

Moreover, power without authority permits leaders of a team to dominate employees by denying legitimacy to employees' needs and desires. In the Subaru-Isuzu plant, where the managers used the sports metaphor of calling themselves coaches, Laurie Graham found it was difficult, if not fatal, for a worker to talk straight to a boss-coach about problems in terms other than team cooperation; straight talk involving demands for higher pay or less pressure to boost productivity was seen as a lack of employee cooperativeness. The good team player doesn't whine. Fictions of teamwork, because of their very superficiality of content and focus on the immediate moment, their avoidance of resistance and deflection of confrontation, are thus useful in the exercise of domination. Deeper shared commitments, loyalties, and trust would require more time—and for that very reason would not be as manipulable. The manager who declares that we are all victims of time and place is perhaps the most cunning figure to appear in the pages of this book. He has mastered the art of wielding power without being held accountable; he has transcended that responsibility for himself, putting the ills of work back on the shoulders of those fellow "victims" who happen to work for him.

This game of power without authority indeed begets a new character type. In place of the driven man, there appears the ironic man. Richard Rorty writes of irony that it is a state of mind in which people are "never quite able to take themselves seriously because always aware that the terms in which they describe themselves are subject to change, always aware of the contingency and fragility of their final vocabularies, and thus of their selves."[106] An ironic view of oneself is the logical consequence of living in flexible time, without standards of authority and accountability. Yet Rorty understands that no society can cohere through irony; about education, he declares, "I cannot imagine a culture which socialized its youth in such a way as to make them continually dubious about their own process of socialization."[107] Nor does irony stimulate people to challenge power; he says this sense of self will not make "you better able to conquer the forces which are marshaled against you."[108] Ironic character, of the sort Rorty describes, becomes self-destructive in the modern world; one moves from believing nothing is fixed to "I am not quite real, my needs have no substance." There is no one, no authority, to recognize their worth.

THE ETHOS OF TEAMWORK, with its inner suspensions and ironies, takes us far away from the moral universe of Virgil's grim, heroic farmer. And the power relations contained in teamwork, power exercised without claims to authority, is far distant from the ethics of self-responsibility which marked the old work ethic, with its deadly-serious, worldly asceticism. The classic work ethic of delayed gratification and proving oneself through hard labor can hardly claim our affections. But teamwork should have no greater claim, in its fictions and its feigning of community.

Neither the old nor the new work ethic provides a satisfactory answer to Pico della Mirandola's question "How should I fashion my life?" Pico's question indeed brings to a head all the issues we have pursued about time and character in the new capitalism.

The culture of the new order profoundly disturbs self-organization. It can divorce flexible experience from static personal ethics, as happened to Rico. It can divorce easy, superficial labor from understanding and engagement, as happened to the Boston bakers. It can make the constant taking of risks an exercise in depression, as happened to Rose. Irreversible change and multiple, fragmented activity may be comfortable for the new regime's masters, like the court at Davos, but it may disorient the regime's servants. And the new cooperative ethos of teamwork sets in place as masters those "facilitators" and "process managers" who dodge truthful engagement with their servants.

In drawing this picture I am well aware it risks, despite all qualifications, appearing as a contrast between before, which was better, and now, which is worse. None of us could desire to return to the security of Enrico's or the Greek bakers' generation. It was claustrophobic in outlook; its terms of self-organization were rigid. In a longer-term view, while the achievement of personal security has served a profound practical as well as psychological need in modern capitalism, that achievement carried a high price. A deadening politics of seniority and time entitlements ruled the unionized workers at Willow Run; to continue that mind-set today would be a recipe for self-destruction in today's markets and flexible networks. The problem we confront is how to organize our life histories now, in a capitalism which disposes us to drift.

The dilemma of how to organize a life narrative is partly clarified by probing how, in today's capitalism, people cope with the future.

SEVEN

Failure

Failure is the great modern taboo. Popular literature is full of recipes for how to succeed, but largely silent about how to cope with failure. Coming to terms with failure, giving it a shape and a place in one's life history, may haunt us internally but seldom is discussed with others. Instead we reach for the safety of clichés; champions of the poor do so when they seek to deflect the lament "I have failed" by the supposedly healing reply "No you haven't; you are a victim." As with anything we are afraid to speak about forthrightly, both internal obsession and shame only thereby become greater. Left untreated is the raw inner sentence "I am not good enough."

Failure is no longer the normal prospect facing only the very poor or disadvantaged; it has become more familiar as a regular event in the lives of the middle classes. The shrinking size of the elite makes achievement more elusive. The winner-take-all market is a competitive structure which disposes large numbers of educated people to fail. Downsizings and reengineerings impose on middle-class people sudden disasters which were in an earlier capitalism much more confined to the working classes. The sense of failing one's family by behaving flexibly and adaptively at work, such as haunts Rico, is more subtle but equally powerful.

The very opposition of success and failure is one way of avoiding coming to terms with failure itself. This simple division suggests that if we have enough evidence of material achievement we won't be haunted by feelings of insufficiency or inadequacy—which wasn't the case for Weber's driven man, who felt that whatever is, is not enough. One of the reasons it is hard to assuage feelings of failure with dollars is that failure can be of a deeper kind—failure to make one's life cohere, failure to realize something precious in oneself, failure to live rather than merely exist. Failure can occur when Pico's journey is aimless and endless.

On the eve of the First World War, the commentator Walter Lippmann, unhappy with the reckoning of success in dollars which preoccupied his contemporaries, pondered their unsettled lives in a vigorous book he called *Drift and Mastery.* He sought to transmute the material reckoning of failure and success into more personal experiences of time, opposing drifting, erratic experience to mastery of events.

Lippmann lived in the era when the giant industrial firms of America and Europe consolidated. Everyone knows the evils of this capitalism, Lippmann said: the death of small firms, the collapse of government conducted in the name of the public good, the masses fed into the capitalist maw. The problem with his fellow reformers, Lippmann observed, is that they "knew what they were against but not what they were for."[109] People suffered, they complained, but neither the nascent Marxist program nor renewed individual enterprise offered a promising remedy. The Marxists proposed a massive social explosion, the individual entrepreneurs greater freedom to compete; neither was a recipe for an alternative *order.* Lippmann, however, was in no doubt over what to do.

Surveying the resolute, hardworking determination of the immigrants then swelling America, he proclaimed in a memorable phrase, "All of us are immigrants spiritually."[110] The personal qualities of resolve invoked by Hesiod and Virgil, Lippmann saw embodied again in the relentless hard work of immigrants on New York's Lower East Side. What Lippmann hated was the sensitive aesthete's distaste for capitalism, personified, he thought, in Henry James, who looked at the New York immigrants as an alien if energetic race, disheveled and anarchic in their struggles.[111]

What should guide people, cut loose from home, now trying to create a new life narrative? For Lippmann, it was the conduct of a career. Not to make a career out of one's work, however modest its content or its pay, was to leave oneself prey to the sense of aimlessness which constitutes the deepest experience of inadequacy—one must, in modern slang, "get a life." Thus he recovered the oldest meaning of career, which I cited at the opening of this essay, career as a well-made road. Cutting that road was the antidote to personal failure.

Can we practice this remedy for failure in flexible capitalism? Though we may think today of a career as synonymous with the professions, one of its elements—the possession of skill—has not been limited to the professional or even bourgeois realm. The historian Edward Thompson points out that in the nineteenth century even the least favored workers, whether poorly employed, unemployed, or simply foraging from job to job, tried to define themselves as weavers, metalworkers, or farmers.[112] Status in work comes from being more than just "a pair of hands"; manual laborers as well as upper servants in Victorian households sought it in using the words "career," "profession," and "craft" more indiscriminately than we might think admissible. The desire for such status was equally potent among middle-class employees of the new corporations; as the historian Olivier Zunz has shown, people in the business world first sought in Lippmann's era to elevate their work by treating accounting, salesmanship, or managing as akin to the doctor's or engineer's professional activities.[113]

The desire for the status of a career is thus nothing new. Nor is the sense that careers, rather than jobs, develop our characters. But Lippmann raised the stakes of "getting a life." In Lippmann's view, the life narrative of a career is a story of inner development, unfolding through both skill and struggle. "We have to deal with [life] deliberately, devise its social organization, alter its tools, formulate its method. . . ."[114] The person pursuing a career defines long-term purposes, standards of professional or unprofessional behavior, and a sense of responsibility for his or her conduct. I doubt Lippmann had read Max Weber when he wrote *Drift and Mastery*; the two writers, though, shared a similar concept of career. In Weber's usage, *Beruf,* which is the German equivalent for "career," also stresses the importance of work as a narrative and the development of character possible only by long-term, organized effort. "Mastery means," Lippmann declares, "the substitution of conscious intention for unconscious striving."[115]

Lippmann's generation believed that they stood at the beginning of a new age of science as well as of capitalism. They were convinced that the proper use of science, technical skills, and, more generally, professional knowledge could help men and women to form stronger career histories, and thus to take firmer control of their own lives. In this reliance on science for personal mastery Lippmann resembled other progressive contemporaries in America, and Fabian socialists like Sidney and Beatrice Webb in Britain, or the young Leon Blum in France, as well as Max Weber.

Lippmann's recipe for mastery also had a specific political aim. He observed the New York immigrants struggling to learn English and to educate themselves in order to begin their careers, but shut out of the institutions of higher learning in the city, which at the time were closed to Jews and blacks and hostile to Greeks, Italians, and the Irish. In calling for a more career-oriented society, he was demanding that these institutions open their doors, an American version of the French motto "careers open to talent."

Lippmann's writing constitutes a massive act of faith in the individual, in making something of *oneself*—Pico's dream, brought to life on the streets of the Lower East Side among people Lippmann saw as particular, distinctive human beings. In his writings Lippmann thus tended to pit the Goliath of corporate capitalism against the David of personal will and talent.

The pleasures of reading Lippmann are their own justification; his voice is that of an upright, clean-living Edwardian

schoolteacher who has seemingly also spent many hours on
picket lines or in the company of men whose words he can
barely understand. Still, is his belief in career a viable prescription for us, nearly a century later? In particular, is it a
remedy for failure—failure of the sort which consists of aimlessness, of not getting one's life together?

We know different forms of bureaucracy from those Lippmann and Weber knew; capitalism now acts on different productive principles. The short-term, flexible time of the new
capitalism seems to preclude making a sustained narrative out
of one's labors, and so a career. Yet to fail to wrest some sense
of continuity and purpose out of these conditions would be literally to fail ourselves.

LIPPMANN HAS OFTEN BEEN on my mind in attending to a group
of middle-aged programmers I've come to know, men who recently were downsized at an American IBM office. Before they
lost their jobs, they—rather complacently—subscribed to belief in the long-term unfolding of their professional careers. As
high-tech programmers, they were meant to be the masters of
the new science. After they were let go, they had to try out different interpretations of the events which wrecked their lives;
they could summon no self-evident, instant narrative which
would make sense of their failure. And yet, by means Lippmann perhaps did not foresee, they've rescued themselves
from the sense of aimless drift, and indeed found in their very
failure a certain revelation of their life career.

Let me first set their company context, since it is distinctive.
Up to the mid-1980s, IBM practiced paternal capitalism with a
vengeance.[116] The man responsible for IBM's growth, Thomas
Watson, Sr., ran the company like a personal fief and spoke of
himself as the "moral father" of the firm. The old company song
went, "With Mr. Watson leading, To greater heights we'll rise,
And keep our IBM, Respected in all eyes."[117] The company was
run like an army, and Watson's personal decisions about all aspects of the corporation became instant company law. "Loyalty," he said, "saves the wear and tear of making daily decisions

as to what is best to do."[118] Institutionally, IBM resembled a state-run company in France or Italy, with lifetime employment for most employees and a kind of social contract between management and labor.

In 1956, Thomas Watson, Jr., took over from his father. He delegated more and listened better, but the social contract remained in force. IBM gave its workers excellent health insurance, education and pension benefits; it supported workers' social lives with company golf courses, child care, and mortgages; above all, it provided a lifetime ladder of employment, all the stages of a career laid out for people who were expected to stay and to climb. IBM could do so because it exercised a near monopoly in its markets.

Due to grave miscalculations about the growth of the computer industry in the 1980s—IBM virtually threw away its control of the personal computer—by the early 1990s the company was in the throes of upheaval. Watson Jr. had retired; new chairmen foundered. In 1992 the firm suffered a massive loss ($6.6 billion), whereas eight years before it had racked up the largest American corporate profit on record. An elaborate internal bureaucracy had proved immobilizing as the company was outmaneuvered by Bill Gates's Microsoft. IBM also faced stiff competition from Japanese and American upstarts. In 1993, it began, with yet another new chairman, Louis Gerstner, to fashion itself into a competitive corporate machine, and made an equally dramatic turnaround. It sought to replace the rigid hierarchical structure of work with more flexible forms of organization, and with flexible production oriented to getting more products more quickly to market.

The tenure of its 400,000 workers was a prime target in this campaign. At first some were enticed, then many more were forced to go. In the first six months of 1993, a third of the employees in the three IBM plants located in the Hudson Valley in New York were laid off, and the company downsized other operations wherever possible. The new management closed the golf courses and clubs and withdrew from supporting the communities in which IBM operated.

I wanted to know more about what this great turn toward a leaner, more flexible IBM was like, in part because many of the managers and middle-aged engineers caught in the change are my neighbors in upstate New York. Made redundant at a too early age, they have carved out employment as "consultants," which means working their address books in the often vain hope that contacts outside the corporation still remember they exist. Some have gone back to work for the corporation, but as short-term workers on contracts, lacking company benefits and standing in the institution. However they've managed to survive the last four years, they can't live without attending to the brute facts of corporate change and its effects on their own lives.

The River Winds Café, not far from my neighbors' old offices, is a cheery hamburger joint, formerly tenanted during daylight hours only by women out shopping or sullen adolescents wasting time after school. It is here that I've heard these white-shirted, dark-tied men, who nurse cups of coffee while sitting attentively as if at a business meeting, sort out their histories. One knot of five to seven men sticks together; they were mainframe programmers and systems analysts in the old IBM. The most talkative among them were Jason, a systems analyst who had been with the company nearly twenty years, and Paul, a younger programmer whom Jason had fired in the first downsizing wave.

I began spending occasional late afternoons with them in 1994, a year after all but Jason had been let go and a year after I'd met Rico on the flight to Vienna. At the River Winds Café, the engineers' attempt to make sense of what had happened fell roughly into three stages. When I entered the discussions, the men felt themselves passive victims of the corporation. But by the time the discussions came to a conclusion, the dismissed employees had switched focus to their own behavior.

When the pain of dismissal was still raw, discussion revolved around IBM's "betrayals," as if the company had tricked them. The programmers dredged up corporate events or behavior in the past that seemed to portend the changes which subsequently came to pass. These acts of recall included such bits of evidence as a particular engineer's being denied use of the golf-course for a full eighteen rounds, or unexplained trips by a head programmer to unnamed destinations. At this stage the men wanted evidence of premeditation on the part of their superiors, evidence which would then justify their own sense of outrage. Being tricked or betrayed means a disaster is hardly one's own fault.

Indeed, the sense of corporate betrayal struck most outside observers who came to the company at the time. It was a dramatic story: highly skilled professionals in a paternalistic company now treated with no more regard than lowly clerks or janitors. The company seemed to have wrecked itself in the process. The English journalist Anthony Sampson, who visited the company's home offices in the mid-1990s, found social disorganization rife within the company, rather than a reinvigorated workforce. One official admitted, "There's much more stress, domestic violence and need for mental services—directly linked to the layoffs. Even inside IBM the environment has changed radically: they have great unease, without their security."[119] People who had survived behaved as though they lived on borrowed time, feeling they had survived for no good reason. As for the dismissed, a local pastor and former IBM worker commented to Sampson, "They feel bitter and betrayed. . . . we were made to feel as if we were the cause of their failure, while the big guys were making millions."

Paul Carroll, another student of this debacle, reports that on an anonymous employee morale survey, one person responded to the company's new insistence on its respect for individual effort rather than corporate loyalty, "What respect? . . . IBM is a very inconsistent company, making grand public statements on respect, sincerity, and sensitivity while practicing oppressive, discriminatory administration at a lower level." "Corporate loyalty is dead," a management consultant flatly declared.[120] And at ATT, a sister corporate monster which went through the same process, there was, in the words of one executive, "a climate of fear. There was fear in the old days too, but when they cut 40,000 jobs who is going to criticize a supervisor?"[121]

But in the River Winds Café these first reactions didn't hold. The programmers found that as an explanation, *premeditated* betrayal wouldn't wash logically. For one thing, many of the superiors who fired them in the early phases of corporate restructuring were themselves fired in later phases; like Jason, they could also now be found at the River Winds. Again, since the company was in fact doing badly through much of the 1980s and early 1990s, the unpalatable facts were all too amply recorded in its annual balance sheet; the dysfunctions of the old corporate culture were plainly on display, rather than hidden.

Most of all, as reasonable adults the programmers came to understand that the theory of betrayal, planned or unplanned, converted the bosses into stick figures of evil. When Paul cited for the fourth or fifth time the mysterious trips of the head programmer, the other people at the table finally jumped on him. "Come on," Jason said, "you know he was a decent guy. He was probably visiting his girlfriend. No one knew what was coming." To this proposition, others had come to agree. And the effect of this consensus was to make the ills of the corporate albatross more real in fact than in fantasy.

So in a second stage of interpretation they focused on finding external forces to blame. At the River Winds Café, the "global economy" now appeared the source of their misfortunes, particularly in its use of foreign workers. IBM had begun "outsourcing" some of its programming work, paying people in India a fraction of the wages paid to the Americans. The cheap wages paid to these foreign professionals were cited as a reason the company had made the Americans redundant. More surprisingly, the company's communications network served as something like the Indians' Ellis Island, their port of immigration, since code written in Amenadabab arrived on a supervisor's desk as rapidly as code written in-house. (In this regard, Jason told me a rather a paradoxical fact he had learned from survivors of his own wave of downsizing: people in this high-tech company rarely put on-line their judgments or criticisms; they wanted to leave no traces for which they could be held accountable.)

The fear that foreigners undermine the efforts of hardworking native Americans is a deeply rooted one. In the nineteenth century, it was very poor, unskilled immigrant workers who seemed to take away jobs, by their willingness to work for less. Today, the global economy serves the function of arousing this ancient fear, but those threatened at home seem not just the unskilled, but also the middle classes and professionals caught up in the flux of the global labor market. Many American physicians have cited, for example, the flood of "cheap doctors" from Third World countries as one of the reasons their own security can be menaced by insurers and health-maintenance companies. Economists like Lester Thurow have sought to generalize this threat, in arguing that the shift of work to low-wage sites around the world drags down wages in advanced economies like the United States. Rationally, this fear of the global labor market can be debated; Paul Krugman points out, for instance, that only 2 percent of the national income in America comes from imports from low-wage economies elsewhere in the world. But the belief in personal jeopardy caused by external threat is deep-seated and discounts fact.

For instance, in this "protectionist" phase of the discussion, which lasted for several months, the men at the café sought to explain their own troubles by equating foreign influence and American "outsiders" taking over the corporation: they noted repeatedly the fact that the new president of IBM, Louis Gerstner, was Jewish. Unfortunately this phase occurred during the elections of 1994; several of the men voted for extreme right-wing candidates whom they would have found absurd in more secure times.

Yet again, though, this shared interpretation would not hold. The turning point in rejecting the perfidy of outsiders came when the employees first began to discuss their own careers, particularly their professional values. As scientist-engineers, the programmers believed in the virtues of technological developments like digital global communications. They also acknowledged the quality of the work coming out of India.

These acknowledgments meant more than paying abstract obeisance to professional standards. The fact that the men were talking together mattered. During the stage in which the programmers constructed the perfidy of the Indian wage-busters and the machinations of IBM's Jewish president, the men had little to share with one another about the content of their work. Silences frequently fell over the table; betrayal within the company and external victimization both kept talk within the confines of complaining. Focusing on external enemies indeed gave the programmers no professional standing at all. The story referred only to the actions of others, unknown and unseen elsewhere; the engineers became passive agents of global forces.

Jim, the oldest of the IBM employees, and therefore the one who has had the most trouble reestablishing himself, remarked to me, "You know, during the Korean War, I thought, 'I'm just a pawn, no one, in this mud.' But I became more of a pawn at IBM." As the third stage of intepetation began, Paul, who had once suspected the perfidy of a voyaging superior, rounded on Jim, whom he greatly admired. He reminded Jim that they hadn't just been putting in their hours at IBM. Sure, once they had believed in the company, but even more to the point, Paul said, "we love our work." To which Jim replied, "That's quite true. I still love doing it—when I can." And so gradually the men began to speak in a different way.

This third stage of explanation restored some of their sense of integrity as programmers, but at a high cost. Now the focus was more on the history of high-tech work, on its immense recent growth, on the skills needed to deal with industrial and scientific challenges. Something happened to the voices of the men speaking at the café as they abandoned their obsession with how they had been hurt by others. As they focused on the profession, the programmers began to speak about what they personally could and should have done earlier in their own careers in order to prevent their present plight. In this third stage, the discourse of career had finally appeared, career as Walter Lippmann might have imagined it. Matters of personal will and choice, professional standards, narratives of work, all emerged—save that the theme of this career discourse was failure rather than mastery.

These discussions were indeed premised on the fact that IBM had stayed committed to mainframe computers at a time when growth in the industry occurred in the personal-computer sector; most of the programmers were mainframe men. The IBM men began to blame themselves for having been too company-dependent, for having believed in the promises of corporate culture, for having played out a career scenario not of their own creation. "Blame" may suggest guilt. I didn't hear that in the men's voices, at least not guilt of the florid, self-pitying sort. The talk was of mainframes, workstations, the possibilities of Java, the problems of bandwidth—and self. In this third stage, the unemployed recited the successes of people who ten or twelve years ago went into the personal-computer sector via risky small businesses, or who foresaw the possibilities of the Internet. This is what the programmers at the River Winds Café think they should have done. They should have become entrepreneurs like kids in Silicon Valley, the home of small technology start-ups.

"We had the example," Kim, a network specialist, declared one day. "We knew everything going on out on the [West] Coast, and we did nothing." All but Jim nodded agreement; he mentioned the problem of raising capital. "Nonsense," Kim replied. "This business isn't about today, it's about what might happen. You get money for that." The history of IBM's internal blunders, the corporate reorganization motivated by the desire for flexibility, the advent of the global labor market evinced by the Indian programmers—all were rearranged as signals that it was time to get out. They should have taken the risk.

For the last year, the story of what happened to IBM and to

them has rested here. And this last interpretation, I've noticed, has coincided with a change in my neighbors' behavior in the community. Formerly town aldermen and school board members, they have now dropped out from pursuing these offices. They aren't afraid of holding up their heads in the community, since so many people in our town have been dismissed by IBM or suffered financially as shop owners and tradesmen from the shake-up. They've just lost interest in civic affairs.

The one community engagement the men do keep up, indeed pursue with ever greater vigor, is membership in and stewardship of their local churches. This is important to them because of the personal contact they have with other church members. In this part of the countryside as elsewhere, fundamentalist and evangelical forms of Christianity have been sharply on the rise. The youngest, Paul, told me, "When I was born again in Christ, I became more accepting, less striving." If my neighbors have taken responsibility for their life histories, that ethical act has taken their conduct in a particular direction; they have turned inward.

A SUCCESSFUL ENTREPRENEUR from Silicon Valley reading this account might well comment, "This shows indeed that they should have taken more risks. Once these men understood the nature of a modern career, they were right to hold themselves accountable. They failed to act." Of course, that harsh judgment assumes the programmers were endowed with foresight. Even so, the discussions at the River Winds Café could thus be taken simply as a cautionary tale about the aggravated vulnerability built into careers today.

But to leave the matter here would exclude the real work these men were engaged in: facing up to their failure, making sense of it in terms of their own characters. In an interview Michel Foucault gave shortly before he died, the philosopher asked his interviewer a question: how does one "govern oneself"?

> How does one "govern oneself" by performing actions in which
> one is oneself the object of those actions, the domains in which
> they are applied, the instruments to which they have recourse
> and the subject which acts?[122]

The programmers needed to answer that question by finding
ways to confront the reality of failure and self-limits. That effort of interpretation is also in Lippmann's spirit of "mastery,"
of ceasing to suffer change passively and blindly. To be sure,
the action they take is talking to each other. But it's real action
nonetheless. They are breaking the taboo on failure, bringing
it out into the open. For this reason, the way they talk is important to understand.

The men try out three stories. All three versions revolve
around a crucial turning point; in the first the turning point
occurs when existing management begins to betray the professionals, in the second when intruders arrive on the scene,
in the third at the moment when the programmers fail to get
out. None takes the form of a story in which personal disaster
is long and slow in the making, from the time of Thomas
Watson, Sr., onward.

Shaping a narrative around sudden, crucial moments of
change is, of course, a familiar convention of both novels and
autobiographies. In his *Confessions,* for instance, Jean-
Jacques Rousseau declares, apropos of a whipping he received
as a boy from Mlle. Lambercier, "Who could have supposed
that this childish punishment, received at the age of eight at
the hands of a woman of thirty, would determine my tastes
and desires, my passions, my very self for the rest of my
life?"[123] This marker of change helps Rousseau define a shape
for his life history, despite the wild flux inside himself, as when
he declares that "there are times when I am so unlike myself
that I might be taken for someone else of an entirely opposite
character."[124] The convention of the crucial moment is a way
of making change legible and clear, rather than messy, blind,
or merely a spontaneous combustion. The latter sort of
change appears in Goethe's autobiography: deciding to aban-

don his past life, Goethe says of himself, "Where he is going, who knows? Scarcely can he remember whence he came!"[125]

As for Rousseau, the convention of the defining, clarifying moment helps the programmers make sense of the shape of their careers. Their discussions were, of course, not three neat, well-made chapters; relaxed chat inevitably wanders and weaves. But in the first two versions, nagging truths get in the way of the defining events. The first version is deflated by the men's factual knowledge of IBM's condition, the second by the men's belief in technological progress and their sense of professional quality. The third version, however, frees the people talking to take control of the narrative. Now the story can flow: it has a solid center, "me," and a well-made plot "What I should have done was take my life into my own hands." The defining moment occurs when the programmers switch from passive victimhood to a more active condition. Now their own actions matter to the story. Being fired is no longer the defining event of the third version; the crucial action is the action they should have taken in 1984 or 1985. That defining moment becomes their own responsibility. It is only by making this shift that they can begin to face the fact they've failed in their careers.

The taboos surrounding failure mean that it is often a deeply confusing, ill-defined experience. A single, sharp blow of rejection won't contain failure. In a superb study of the downwardly mobile middle-class, the anthropologist Katherine Newman observes that "despite its various outcomes, managerial downward mobility generates a floating, ambiguous, liminal condition." To be a downwardly mobile executive, she says, "is first to discover that you are not as good a person as you thought you were and then to end up not sure who or what you are."[126] The men at the River Winds Café eventually rescued themselves from that subjective ambiguity.

It might appear that this narrative working out of failure is arbitrary. Nietzsche says in *Thus Spake Zarathustra* that the ordinary man is an angry spectator of the past, and lacks the power to "will backwards."[127] The programmers could not live as angry spectators of their past, however, and so they indeed bent their wills backward in time. And in the evolution of the narrative the men at the River Winds Café eventually ceased to speak as the children of a paternalistic company: they let go of the view that the powerful are scheming demons, their Bombay replacements illegitimate intruders. Their interpretation became in these ways more realistic.

How does this narrative *form* break the sense of aimless inner drift which Lippmann thought so corrosive? Consider another kind of narrative which might be better attuned to contemporary circumstances. The novelist Salman Rushdie asserts that the modern self is "a shaky edifice we build out of scraps, dogmas, childhood injuries, newspaper articles, chance remarks, old films, small victories, people hated, people loved."[128] To him, a life narrative appears as a collage, an assemblage of the accidental, the found, and the improvised. The same emphasis on discontinuity appears in the writings of the philosopher Zygmunt Bauman and the theologian Mark Taylor; they celebrate the efforts of novelists like Joyce or Calvino to subvert well-made plots as a way to render the flow of ordinary experience.[129] The psyche dwells in a state of endless becoming—a selfhood which is never finished. There can be under these conditions no coherent life narrative, no clarifying moment of change illuminating the whole.

Such views of narrative, sometimes labeled "postmodern," indeed mirror the experience of time in the modern political economy. A pliant self, a collage of fragments unceasing in its becoming, ever open to new experience—these are just the psychological conditions suited to short-term work experience, flexible institutions, and constant risk-taking. But there is little room for understanding the breakdown of a career, if you believe that all life history is just an assemblage of fragments. Nor is there any room for assaying the gravity and pain of failure, if failure is just another incident.

The fragmentation of narrative time is particularly marked in the programmers' professional milieu. In *City of Bits,* the architect William Mitchell describes cyberspace as like "a city unrooted to any definite spot on the surface of the earth . . . and inhabited by disembodied and fragmented subjects who exist as collections of aliases and agents."[130] The technology analyst Sherry Turkle describes a young person telling her, "I just turn on one part of my mind and then another when I go from window to window. I'm in some kind of argument in one window and trying to come on to a girl . . . in another, and another window might be running a spreadsheet program."[131]   Fredric Jameson speaks of the "ceaseless rotation of elements" in modern experience, such as occurs in moving through windows onscreen.[132]

The programmers have recovered in talk the connectedness absent onscreen. Their narrative appears indeed pre-postmodern in its striving for coherence and a solid authorial "I." It might be said that theirs is—to use another fashionable phrase—a narrative of resistance. But in its ethical scope the denouement of this talk was more profound.

The programmers spoke in the end with an air more of resigned finality than of anger about being "past it," about having blown their chances, even though they are in their physical prime. In this third version, the men felt relieved of struggling anymore—felt a deep-seated fatigue with life which overcomes many middle-aged people. Anyone who has deeply tasted failure will recognize the impulse: given the destruction of hope and desire, the preservation of one's own active voice is the only way to make failure bearable. Simply declaring one's will to endure will not suffice. Rico is full of guiding principles, and has plenty of absolute advice to give himself, but these nostrums don't heal his fears. The advice the engineers give to themselves consists of such locutions as "I should have known . . ." and "if only . . ." In this diction, relief is no stranger to resignation. And resignation is an acknowledgment of the weight of objective reality.

Their narrative thus attempted a kind of self-healing. Narrative in general does the work of healing through its structure, however, not through offering advice. Even great allegories, even those so unashamed in moralizing as Bunyan's *Pilgrim's Progress*, transcend the intent to show a reader how to act.

Bunyan, for example, makes the temptations of evil so compli-cated that the reader dwells on Christian's difficulties rather than seeks to imitate his solutions. The healing of narrative comes from precisely that engagement with difficulty. The healing work of making a narrative does not limit its interest to events coming out the "right" way. Instead a good narrative ac-knowledges and probes the reality of all the wrong ways life can and does turn out. The reader of a novel, the spectator at a play, experiences the particular comfort of seeing people and events fit into a pattern of time; the "moral" of narrative lies in the form, not in advice.

It could be said, finally, that these men have confronted fail-ure in the past, elucidated the values of their careers, but found no way to go forward. In the flexible, fragmented pre-sent it may seem possible only to create coherent narratives about what has been, and no longer possible to create predic-tive narratives about what will be. The fact that the men at the River Winds Café have withdrawn now from active engage-ment in the local community may seem only to confirm this past-tense condition. The flexible regime may seem to beget a character structure constantly "in recovery."

Ironically, these are the Davids confronting a Goliath of the flexible regime. It is as individuals of the sort Walter Lippmann admired that programmers found a way to discuss failure with each other, and thereby find a more coherent sense of self and time. While we should admire that individual strength, their turn inward and to intimate relations shows the limits of the coherence they achieved. A larger sense of community, and a fuller sense of character, is required by the increasing number of people who, in modern capitalism, are doomed to fail.

EIGHT

The Dangerous Pronoun

The most persuasive practical proposals I've heard for coping with the problems of the new capitalism focus on the places where it operates. Modern corporations like to present themselves as having cut free from the claims of place; a factory in Mexico, an office in Bombay, a media center in lower Manhattan—these appear as mere nodes in the global network. Today, localities, cities, or nations fear that if they exercise their sovereignty, for instance by imposing taxes or restraining summary firings, a corporation could as easily find another island in the network, a factory in Canada if not Mexico, an office in Boston if not Manhattan. From fear of provoking IBM to leave altogether, many localities in the Hudson Valley held back from challenging its decision to devastate the work lives of citizens like the programmers.

Already, though, there are signs that the economy is not as indifferent to location as has been assumed: you can buy any stock you like in Dubuque, Iowa, but not make a market in stocks in the cornfields. IBM was in fact too rooted in its network of suppliers and distributors, in its proximity to the financial activities in New York City, simply to flee abroad. As the political economist Saskia Sassen has observed, the global economy does not float in outer space. Even in the most flexible labor markets on the globe, in Southeast Asia, it is becoming clear that local social and cultural geographies count for a great deal in particular investment decisions.[133] Place has power, and the new economy might be restrained by it.

Is it more effective to challenge the new capitalism from without, in the places where it operates, or seek to reform its operations from within? Of the three structural aspects of flexibility—discontinuous reinvention, flexible production, and concentration of power without centralization—it seems indeed possible to curb from the outside some destructive consequences of discontinuous reinvention; downsizing could be limited, for instance. It would be harder to regulate the others externally. But restraint alone is the wrong issue.

The effort to control the workings of the new capitalism from without has to have a different rationale: it must ask what value is the corporation to the community, how does it serve civic interests rather than just its own ledger of profit and loss? Imposing external standards of behavior often begets internal reform; precisely because the network-world is so amorphous, so inconstant, external standards of responsible behavior may hold up to the corporation a picture of "what you should be like, here, where you are, right now." However, the aim to make corporations better citizens, though worthy, also has its limits. The new owners of the Boston bakery, for instance, act indeed as good citizens, sharing both their profits and their personnel; Rodney Everts, who sought in vain to teach his coworkers baking, is released a day each week from work to teach baking in a local technical school. Yet this act of civic goodwill does nothing inside the bakery to make labor more engaging, nor does it strengthen the work identities of Everts's employees.

Place is geography, a location for politics; community evokes the social and personal dimensions of place. A place becomes a community when people use the pronoun "we." To speak in this way requires a particular though not a local attachment; a nation can constitute a community when in it people translate shared beliefs and values into concrete, daily practices. Rousseau was the first modern writer to understand how deeply the workings of politics are founded on these rituals of everyday life, how much politics depends on the communal "we." One of the unintended consequences of modern capitalism is that it has strengthened the value of place, aroused a longing for community. All the emotional conditions we have explored in the workplace animate that desire: the uncertainties of flexibility; the absence of deeply rooted trust and commitment; the superficiality of teamwork; most of all, the specter of failing to make something of oneself in the world, to "get a life" through one's work. All these conditions impel people to look for some other scene of attachment and depth.

Today, in the new regime of time, that usage "we" has become an act of self-protection. The desire for community is defensive, often expressed as rejection of immigrants or other outsiders—the most important communal architecture being the walls against a hostile economic order. To be sure, it is almost a universal law that "we" can be used as a defense against confusion and dislocation. Current politics based on this desire for refuge takes aim more at the weak, those who travel the circuits of the global labor market, rather than at the strong, those institutions which set poor workers in motion or make use of their relative deprivation. The IBM programmers, as we've seen, eventually turned inward psychologically, but in one important way they transcended this defensive sense of community, when they ceased blaming their Indian peers and their Jewish president.

"We" is often a false locution when used as a point of reference against the outside world. Rico knew both sides of this false locution only too well. On the one hand he observed that his neighbors, each time he moved, had weak ties to one another; he was meant to start afresh in each of the bedroom suburbs he passed through, places in which people appear and disappear every three or four years. And his own sense of "we," expressed in the language of community standards and family values, was a static abstraction, whose very content he had hated in the past and could not practice in the present. "We" can more largely hide the ill-fitting assemblage of ethnicities in a country, or its histories of internal conflict. Now this fictive "we" has come to life again, to defend against a vigorous new form of capitalism.

For all this, the dangerous pronoun can also be used to explore more searchingly and more positively. Take the two elements of the phrase "a shared fate." What sort of sharing is required to resist, rather than to run from, the new political economy? What kind of sustained personal relations in time can be contained in the use of "we"?

THE SOCIAL BOND arises most elementally from a sense of mutual dependence. All the shibboleths of the new order treat dependence as a shameful condition: the attack on rigid bureaucratic hierarchy is meant to free people structurally from dependence; risk-taking is meant to stimulate self-assertion rather than submission to what is given. Within modern corporations, there is no honorable place for service—the very word conjures up the last refuge of the time-server. John Kotter's celebration of consulting as the acme of flexible business behavior supposes that the consultant is beholden to no one. None of these repudiations of dependence as shameful, however, promotes strong bonds of sharing.

Such attitudes are more than psychological prejudices. The attack on the welfare state, begun in the neoliberal, Anglo-American regime and now spreading to other, more "Rhinish" political economies, treats those who are dependent on the state with the suspicion that they are social parasites, rather than truly helpless. The destruction of welfare nets and entitlements is in turn justified as freeing the political economy to behave more flexibly, as if the parasites were dragging down the more dynamic members of society. Social parasites are also seen to lodge deep within the productive body—or at least that is what is conveyed by the contempt for workers who need to be told what to do, who cannot take initiative themselves. The ideology of social parasitism is a powerful disciplinary tool in the workplace; the worker wants to show he or she is not feeding off the labors of others.

A more positive view of dependence would first of all challenge the commonplace opposition of dependence and independence. Almost without thinking we accept contrast between a weak, dependent self and a strong, independent self. But like the contrast between success and failure, this opposition flattens out reality. "The truly self-reliant person proves to be by no means as independent as cultural stereotypes suppose," the psychologist John Bowlby observes; in adult life, a "healthily self-reliant person" is capable of depending on "others when occasion demands and to know on whom it is appropriate to rely."[134] In intimate relations, the fear of becoming dependent on someone else is a failure to trust him or her; instead, one's defenses rule.

Similarly, in many societies there has been little or no shame attached to more public experiences of dependence, where the weak are in need of the strong. The ancient Roman client asked his patron for favors or help as a matter of course, and the patron lost face if he could not take care of those who looked to him. Louis Dumont and Takeo Doi have documented how in Indian and Japanese societies dependence has similarly carried no hint of self-abasement.[135] In early capitalism, as Albert Hirschmann has shown, trust in business relations arose through open acknowledgment of mutual dependence—which is not quite the same as an honorable relation between strong and weak, but still a recognition that alone one is insufficient to support oneself. Jacques Savary, the seventeenth-century author of *Le parfait négotiant,* declared that divine providence wills "that men would trade together and so that the mutual need which they have to help one another would establish ties of friendship among them."[136] And when traders admit to mutual need, Montesquieu observed a century later, "commerce . . . polishes and softens barbarian ways."[137]

Of course, mutual need also governs modern business dealings; if there is no need for another, there is no exchange. And for most people that need is unequal, because in the modern labor market most people work for someone else. The new order has not erased that brute fact of dependence; the rate of full-time self-employment in the United States, for instance, has held steady at about 8.5 percent for the last forty years.

A single sharp failure is the personal experience which brings most people to recognize that in the longer term, they are not sufficient to themselves. What seems most striking in the experience of the IBM programmers is that they came to speak about failure plainly, without guilt or shame. But this result required the presence of others, and drew each closer to the others. Their achievement—which is not too strong a word —is to have arrived at a state in which they were ashamed neither of their mutual need nor of their own inadequacy.

A positive view of self-limits and mutual dependence might appear more the domain of religious ethics than of political economy. But shame about dependence has a practical consequence. It erodes mutual trust and commitment, and the lack of these social bonds threatens the workings of any collective enterprise.

Difficulties of trust take two forms; in one trust is simply absent, in the other there is a more active suspicion of others. Bond of trust, we have seen, develop informally in the cracks and crevices of bureaucracies as people learn on whom they can depend. Bonds of trust are tested when things go wrong and the need for help becomes acute. One of the reasons that the bakers in Boston have such weak solidarity is that they are helpless when the machines break down. The bakers do not believe they can rely on one another in a crisis, and that belief is correct. No one understands the machines; people are streaming in and out on flextime schedules; they have other jobs and other responsibilities. Rather than mutual suspicion, there is an absence of trust; there is no foundation for it. An absence of trust can also be created by the flexible exercise of power. During its years of downsizing, as Anthony Sampson noted, IBM conveyed an absence of trust in its own surviving employees by telling people they were now on their own, no longer the corporation's children. This sends a potent mixed message: we're all pulling together in the crisis; on the other hand, if you don't take care of yourself, we'll do without you.

When people feel it shameful to be needy, they can become more decidedly mistrustful of others. Take Rose's deep ambivalence about the younger women in her advertising agency. Going to work uptown inaugurated a crisis about her age, expressed in how she felt about her clothes, even the shape of her spectacles. She felt ashamed about her looks, but equally ashamed of needing reassurance; she depended on the younger women for reassurance, but when they gave it, she didn't believe them. In the months of talk I had with her, the "patronizing attitude" of these young women came up again and again; she focused on whether she could really believe what they said and how they behaved with her far more than she worried about the team "facilitator," whom she treated as just a slick joke.

It could be said that this is just a matter of one person's injured pride, but I think not. The acid tone of current discussions of welfare needs, entitlements, and safety nets is pervaded by insinuations of parasitism on one side met by the rage of the humiliated on the other. The more shameful one's sense of dependence and self-limits, the more prone one is to the rage of the humiliated. To restore trust in others is a reflexive act; it requires less fear of vulnerability in oneself. But this reflexive act has a social context. Organizations which celebrate independence and autonomy, far from inspiring their employees, can arouse that sense of vulnerability. And social structures which do not positively promote reliance on others in a crisis instill the more neutral, empty absence of trust.

"TRUST," "MUTUAL RESPONSIBILITY," "COMMITMENT" are all words which have come to be owned by the movement called "communitarianism." It wants to strengthen moral standards, to demand of individuals that they sacrifice for others, promising that if people obey common standards they will find a mutual strength and emotional fulfillment they cannot experience as isolated individuals. Communitarianism in my view has a very dubious claim of ownership of trust or commitment; it falsely emphasizes unity as the source of strength in a community and mistakenly fears that when conflicts arise in a community, social bonds are threatened.

A more realistic view of how communities hold together appears in Lewis Coser's classic essay *The Functions of Social Conflict*.[138] Coser argued that people are bound together more by verbal conflict than by verbal agreement, at least immediate agreement. In conflict, they have to work harder at communicating; as often happens in labor or diplomatic negotiations, gradually the ground rules of engagement bind the contending parties together. Coser remarked that differences of views often become sharper and more explicit even though the parties may eventually come to agreement: the scene of conflict becomes a community in the sense that people learn how to listen and respond to one another even as they more keenly feel their differences.

This view of the communal "we" is far deeper than the often superficial sharing of common values such as appears in modern communitarianism, or in Rico's static declarations about family values. The bonds created by internal conflict are far removed from the defensive declarations of communal solidarity which mark the response to economic dislocation today; in Coser's view, there is no community until differences are acknowledged within it. Teamwork, for instance, does not acknowledge differences in privilege or power, and so is a weak form of community; all the members of the work team are supposed to share a common motivation, and precisely that assumption weakens real communication. Strong bonding between people means engaging over time their differences. Rico has had literally too little time in each of the places he's lived to experience community of this sort.

Postmodern views of the self such as those of Salman Rushdie emphasize rupture and conflict, but not communication between fragmented selves. The process view of community is more reflected in current political studies of deliberative democracy, notably in the work of Amy Gutmann and Dennis Thompson, in which the evolving expression of disagreement is taken to bind people more than the sheer declaration of "correct" principles.[139] The process of community conflict mirrors, in social psychology, both cognitive dissonance and focal attention; in a community focal attention is shared. And there is a curious reflection in this view of community of Adam Smith's attack on routine and celebration of sympathy. Routine is a repetitive action, and so has no history, no evolution; sympathy is a sudden bursting out of understanding of another person which comes, Smith says, not right away but only after a long period of resistance or misperception.

The understanding of community as a process unfolding in time appeared in Diderot's *Encyclopedia,* though L'Anglée was no scene of conflict. The rhythms of time Diderot celebrated there, later affirmed in the writings of Anthony Giddens on habit, emphasized gradual evolution as a civilized form of change. The sociologists of dispute and confrontation do not believe sustained verbal conflict is uncivilized; instead it forms a more realistic basis for the connections between people of unequal power or with differing interests.

It might seem that community of this conflict-laden sort is just what a flexible regime should inspire. The ruptures of time, the social disorganization they entail, should force people into articulation and negotiation of their differences, rather than provoke the superficial cooperativeness of teamwork. Even if their superiors try to duck confrontation, the subordinates studied by Harley Shaiken and Laurie Graham should be looking for it.

Of course, those who have the power to avoid responsibility have as well the means to repress dissent. They do so in repressing the power of "voice," as Albert Hirschmann calls it, among older workers, transmuting the voice of experience into a negative sign of aging, of being too involved in the way things have always been done before. But still, why do some people possess the desire for voice; why would they be willing to keep arguing and deliberating, even to their own detriment? The resolve to stay engaged cannot be confined to a sense of institutional injury, or institutional loyalty. Many more are hurt than cry out. To imagine communities willing to confront the new capitalism, we have also to consider strength of character.

IT IS FOR THESE REASONS that the IBM programmers seemed to me the strongest characters I encountered. They took responsibility for their failures and insufficiencies together. That gave them strength; it also provided a narrative frame for their experience. What sort of coherence in time did they acheive?

Some French philosophers have sought to define the willingness to stay engaged by making a distinction between *maintien de soi,* maintenance of oneself, and *constance à soi,* fidelity to oneself: the first sustains an identity over the course of time, the second invokes such virtues as being honest with oneself about one's defects.[140] The maintenance of oneself is a shifting activity, as one's circumstances change and one's experience accumulates; fidelity to oneself, as in being honest about one's faults, ought to be constant, no matter where or what age one is.

Emmanuel Levinas has tried to make clear, though, that *constance à soi* has a social dimension, in terms of being responsible to other people. This is at once a very simple and a complicated notion. Simple because it asserts my sense of self-worth depends on whether others can rely upon me. Complicated because I need to act responsibly, even if I do not know myself, and no matter how confused or indeed shattered my own sense of identity.[141] This was no abstraction for Levinas; during the Second World War, he witnessed thousands of fellow French Jews struggle to act reliably to each other in the face of Nazi and Vichy persecution, even though most before had not shared a strong common identity as Jews.

Levinas's idea of responsibility and self-constancy of character has in turn been elaborated by the philosopher Paul

Ricoeur as follows: "Because someone is counting on me, I am accountable for my action before another."[142] No matter how erratic one's life, one's word must be good. But Ricoeur argues that we can hew to this standard only by imagining constantly that there is a witness to all we do and say, and that, moreover, this witness is not a passive observer, but someone who relies upon us. In order to be reliable, we must feel needed; for us to feel needed, this Other must be needy.

"Who needs me?" is a question of character which suffers a radical challenge in modern capitalism. The system radiates indifference. It does so in terms of the outcomes of human striving, as in winner-take-all markets, where there is little connection between risk and reward. It radiates indifference in the organization of absence of trust, where there is no reason to be needed. And it does so through reengineering of institutions in which people are treated as disposable. Such practices obviously and brutally diminish the sense of mattering as a person, of being necessary to others.

It could be said that capitalism was always thus. But not in the same way. The indifference of the old class-bound capitalism was starkly material; the indifference which radiates out of flexible capitalism is more personal because the system itself is less starkly etched, less legible in form. Enrico knew where he stood; the old Greek bakers had clear pictures, whether true or false, of their friends and enemies. The old habit of Marxism was to treat confusion as a kind of false consciousness; in our circumstances it is an accurate reflection of reality. Thus the personal confusion today about answering the question "Who in society needs me?"

Lack of responsiveness is a logical reaction to the feeling one is not needed. This is as true of flexible work communities as it is of labor markets downsizing middle-aged workers. Networks and teams weaken character—character as Horace first described it, character as a connection to the world, as being necessary for others. Or again, in communal conflicts it is difficult to engage if your antagonist declares, like the ATT manager, "We are all victims of time and place." The Other is missing, and so you are disconnected. Real connections made to others by acknowledging mutual incomprehension are further diminished by communitarianism and moral protectionism—by those clear affirmations of shared values, by the teamwork "we" of shallow community.

The philosopher Hans-Georg Gadamer declares that "the self we are does not possess itself; one could say that [the self] 'happens'" subject to the accidents of time and the fragments of history. Thus "the self-awareness of the individual," Gadamer declares, "is only a flickering in the closed circuit of historical life."[143] This is the problem of character in modern capitalism. There is history, but no shared narrative of difficulty, and so no shared fate. Under these conditions, character corrodes; the question "Who needs me?" has no immediate answer. Even the community of programmers could no longer answer, other than that they needed the others around the table at the River Winds Café.

Yet I had an epiphany of sorts in Davos, listening to the rulers of the flexible realm. "We" is also a dangerous pronoun to them. They dwell comfortably in entrepreneurial disorder, but fear organized confrontation. They of course fear the resurgence of unions, but become acutely and personally uncomfortable, fidgeting or breaking eye contact or retreating into taking notes, if forced to discuss the people who, in their jargon, are "left behind." They know that the great majority of those who toil in the flexible regime are left behind, and of course they regret it. But the flexibility they celebrate does not give, it cannot give, any guidance for the conduct of an ordinary life. The new masters have rejected careers in the old English sense of the word, as pathways along which people can travel; durable and sustained paths of action are foreign territories.

It therefore seemed to me, as I wandered in and out of the conference halls, weaved through the tangle of limousines and police on the mountainous village streets, that this regime might at least lose its current hold over the imaginations and sentiments of those down below. I have learned from my family's bitter radical past; if change occurs it happens on the ground, between persons speaking out of inner need, rather than through mass uprisings. What political programs follow from those inner needs, I simply don't know. But I do know a regime which provides human beings no deep reasons to care about one another cannot long preserve its legitimacy.

APPENDIX
Statistical Tables

TABLE 1. EMPLOYMENT BY SELECTED INDUSTRY,
WITH PROJECTIONS, 1979 TO 2005

INDUSTRY	EMPLOYMENT (1,000)			ANNUAL GROWTH RATE	
	1979	1992	2005 Proj.[1]	1979–92	1992–2005 Proj.[1]
Manufacturing	21,040	18,040	17.523	–1.2	–0.2
Finance, insurance, and real estate	4,975	6,571	7,969	2.2	1.5
Personnel supply services	508	1,649	2,581	9.5	3.5
Computer and data processing services	271	831	1,626	9.0	5.3
Federal government	2,773	2,969	2,815	0.5	–0.4
State and local government	13,174	15,683	19,206	1.4	1.6

[1] Based on assumptions of moderate growth.

Data extracted from U.S. Bureau of the Census, *Statistical Abstract of the United States: 1995* (Washington, D.C.: 1995), p. 417.

TABLE 2. WAGE INEQUALITY AND UNEMPLOYMENT

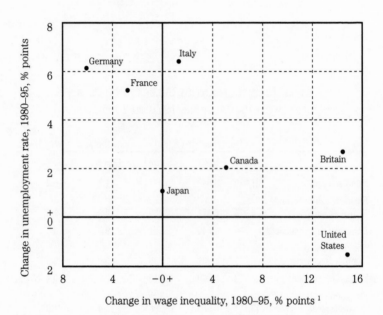

Change in wage inequality, 1980–95, % points [1]

[1] As measured by the ratio of the earnings of the lowest wage decile to the median wage.

Source: OECD

TABLE 3. PRODUCTIVITY GROWTH IN FIVE INDUSTRIALIZED COUNTRIES, 1950–86

PERIOD	FRANCE	GERMANY	JAPAN	UNITED KINGDOM	UNITED STATES
Growth of GDP per Employed Person					
1950–73	4.55	4.99	7.21	2.53	1.96
1973–79	2.65	2.78	2.87	1.30	0.03
1979–86	1.85	1.58	2.72	1.71	0.82
Growth of GDP per Hour, Total Economy					
1950–73	5.01	5.83	7.41	3.15	2.44
1973–79	3.83	3.91	3.40	2.18	0.80
1979–84	3.24	1.88	3.06	2.95	1.09
Growth of GDP per Hour, Manufacturing Sector					
1950–73	5.93	6.31	9.48	3.25	2.62
1973–79	4.90	4.22	5.39	0.83	1.37
1979–86	3.50	2.78	5.47	4.28	3.10

From Martin Neil Baily and Margaret M. Blair, "Productivity and American Management," in Robert E. Litan, Robert Z. Lawrence, and Charles L. Schultze, eds., *American Living Standards: Threats and Challenges* (Washington, D.C.: Brookings Institute, 1988), p. 180.

TABLE 4. U.S. UNION MEMBERSHIP, 1940–93

YEAR	LABOR FORCE[1] (1,000)	UNION MEMBERS (1,000)	PERCENTAGE
1940	32,376	8,717	26.9
1945	40,394	14,322	35.5
1950	45,222	14,267	31.5
1955	50,675	16,802	33.2
1960	54,234	17,049	31.4
1965	60,815	17,299	28.4
1970	70,920	19,381	27.3
1975	76,945	19,611	25.5
1980	90,564	19,843	21.9
1985	94,521	16,996	18.0
1990	103,905	16,740	16.1
1991	102,786	16,568	16.1
1992	103,688	16,390	15.8
1993	105,067	16,598	15.8

[1]Does not include agricultural employment.

Data extracted from *The World Almanac and the Book of Facts, 1995,* (Mahwah, N.J.: 1995), p. 154.

TABLE 5. AGE AND GENDER COMPOSITION OF THE
LABOR FORCE AND RATE OF PART-TIME EMPLOYMENT,
1969, 1979, AND 1989[1]

	1969		1979		1989	
	As % of at-work pop.	% part-time	As % of at-work pop.	% part-time	As % of at-work pop.	% part-time
All 16–21	12.8%	40.6%	14.0%	41.7%	10.3%	46.3%
Women 22–44	17.3	22.7	23.1	22.5	27.7	21.9
Women 45–64	13.2	22.5	11.3	24.4	11.6	23.8
Men 22–64	53.2	3.7	48.9	4.8	47.8	6.7
All 65+	3.5	41.0	2.7	52.9	2.6	52.4
Total	100.0%	15.5%	100.0%	17.6%	100.0%	18.1%

[1] Includes only nonagricultural workers at work.

From Chris Tilly, "Short Hours, Short Shrift: The Causes and Consequences of Part-Time Employment," in Virginia L. duRivage, ed., *New Policies for the Part-Time and Contingent Workforce* (Armonk, N.J.: M. E. Sharpe, 1992), p. 27.

TABLE 6. THE ORGANIZATION OF WORKING TIME IN 1991

CHARACTERISTICS	TOTAL EMPLOY- MENT	WORK SCHEDULES—PERCENT DISTRIBUTION					
		Regular Daytime Schedules		Shift Workers			
		Total	Workers on Flexible[1] Schedules	Total	Evening	Night	Rotating
Total 1991	80,452	81.8	15.1	17.8	5.1	3.7	3.4
Sex							
Male	46,308	79.5	15.5	20.2	5.4	4.2	4.0
Female	34,145	85.0	14.5	14.6	4.6	2.9	2.6
Race & Hispanic Origin							
White	68,795	82.6	15.5	17.1	4.6	3.4	3.3
Black	8,943	76.0	12.1	23.3	8.4	5.6	4.7
Hispanic	6,598	80.3	10.6	19.1	6.4	4.6	2.7
Occupation							
Managerial and professional	22,630	89.6	22.1	10.0	1.6	1.4	1.8
Technical, sales, administration	24,116	85.9	17.7	13.8	3.5	2.4	2.7
Service occupations	8,389	57.1	10.5	42.5	14.7	8.7	7.9
Operators, fabricators, and laborers	13,541	73.4	7.3	26.2	8.6	6.8	4.8

[1] A flexible schedule allows workers to vary the time, and where, they work.

Data extracted from U.S. Bureau of the Census, *Statistical Abstract of the United States: 1995* (Washington, D.C.: 1995), p. 410.

TABLE 7. WORKERS USING COMPUTERS IN WHITE-COLLAR WORK, 1993

		TYPE OF APPLICATION[1]						
CATE-GORY	NO. USING COMPU-TERS (1,000)	Book-keeping/ Inven-tory	Word Process-ing	Communi-cations	Analysis/ Spread-sheets	Data-bases	Desk-top Publish-ing	Sales and Tele-market-ing
Sex								
Male	24,414	41.1	45.2	39.4	35.2	25.3	18.1	40.7
Female	26,692	31.6	44.8	38.1	33.8	19.6	14.5	47.8
Race/Ethnicity								
White	43,020	37.2	45.8	39.3	35.2	23.0	16.7	45.9
Black	4,016	27.5	38.3	37.3	31.2	16.8	12.9	35.5
Hispanic	2,492	29.1	45.6	32.1	27.6	18.7	16.0	33.6
Other	1,578	39.7	39.4	37.2	33.5	22.6	10.2	44.5
Educational Attainment								
Not a H/S graduate	1,190	19.1	54.4	20.4	22.2	9.9	20.6	16.0
H/S graduate	13,307	23.7	52.5	29.4	25.8	13.3	17.6	30.8
Some college	11,548	33.5	49.5	38.5	33.9	20.6	18.0	40.9
Associate degree	5,274	37.5	47.0	39.7	34.7	21.7	14.9	41.6
Bachelor degree	13,162	46.9	40.0	45.1	41.5	28.8	17.0	54.8
Master degree	4,628	47.9	29.3	48.5	41.9	35.3	10.4	63.8
Ph.D. or prof. degree	1,999	42.8	27.9	45.9	39.2	28.3	5.2	66.5

[1]A person may be counted in more than one application.

Data extracted from U.S. Bureau of the Census, *Statistical Abstract of the United States: 1995* (Washington, D.C.: 1995), p. 430.

TABLE 8. EARNINGS OF WORKERS IN THE 1980S ONE TO THREE YEARS AFTER CHANGING THEIR JOBS

EARNINGS	PERCENTAGE OF WORKERS
Not employed when surveyed	27
Earning less than 80% of prior earnings	24
Earning 80–94% of prior earnings	10
Earning 95–104% of prior earnings	11
Earning 105–120% of prior earnings	10
Earning at least 120% of prior earnings	18
TOTAL	100

From Congressional Budget Office, *Displaced Workers: Trends in the 1980s and Implications for the Future* (Washington, D.C.: Congress of the United States, 1990), p. xii.

TABLE 9. EMPLOYMENT AND EDUCATION IN 1990 AND PROJECTED TO 2005

	1990 %	2005 %	% CHANGE
1. Jobs not requiring a college degree	81.0	78.1	–2.9
2. Jobs requiring a college degree	19.0	21.9	2.9
2a. Specific job requiring a college degree			
executive, administrative			
and managerial	5.5	6.2	0.7
professional specialties	9.6	10.8	1.2
technicians	1.0	1.4	0.4
sales representatives and			
supervisors	1.8	2.3	0.5
all other occupations	0.9	1.1	0.2
3. Total number of workers	122,573,000	147,191,000	

Source: Bureau of Labor Statistics, *Monthly Labor Review* 115: 7 (July 1992), p. 15.

TABLE 10. LABOR UNION MEMBERSHIP BY SECTOR, 1983–1994

SECTOR	1983	1985	1990	1994
(Total 1,000)				
Unionized public-sector workers	5,737.2	5,743.1	6,485.0	7,091.0
Unionized private-sector workers	11,980.2	11,253.0	10,254.8	9,649.4
(Percent)				
Unionized public-sector workers	36.7	35.7	36.5	38.7
Unionized private-sector workers	16.5	14.3	11.9	10.8

Data extracted from U.S. Bureau of the Census, *Statistical Abstract of the United States: 1995* (Washington, D.C.: 1995), p. 443.

Notes

1. Quoted in *New York Times*, Feb. 13, 1996, pp. D1, D6.
2. Corporations like Manpower grew 240 percent from 1985 to 1995. As I write, the Manpower firm, with 600,000 people on its payroll, compared with the 400,000 at General Motors and 350,000 at IBM, is now the country's largest employer.
3. James Champy, *Re-engineering Management* (New York: HarperBusiness, 1995) p. 119, pp. 39–40.
4. Walter Powell and Laurel Smith-Doerr, "Networks and Economic Life," in Neil Smelser and Richard Swedberg, eds., *The Handbook of Economic Sociology* (Princeton: Princeton University Press, 1994), p. 381.
5. Ibid.
6. Mark Granovetter, "The Strength of Weak Ties," *American Journal of Sociology* 78 (1973), 1360–80.
7. John Kotter, *The New Rules* (New York: Dutton, 1995) pp. 81, 159.
8. Anthony Sampson, *Company Man* (New York: Random House, 1995), pp. 226–27.
9. Quoted in Ray Pahl, *After Success: Fin de Siècle Anxiety and Identity* (Cambridge, U.K.: Polity Press, 1995), pp. 163–64.
10. The story of these plates is the usual eighteenth-century publishing farrago. Diderot and his coeditor d'Alembert stole many of them from older artists like Réamur or contemporaries like Patte. Cf. John Lough, *The Encyclopédie* (New York: McKay, 1971), pp. 85–90.
11. Herbert Applebaum, *The Concept of Work* (Albany: State University of New York Press, 1992), p. 340.
12. Ibid., p. 379.
13. Adam Smith, *The Wealth of Nations* (1776; London: Methuen,

1961), I:109–12.

14. Ibid., I:353.

15. Ibid., I:302–3.

16. Thomas Jefferson, *Writings*, ed. Merrill D. Peterson (New York: Library of America, 1984), p. 346.

17. James Madison, "Memorial and Remonstrance Against Religious Assessements," quoted in Marvin Meyers, ed., *The Mind of the Founder*, rev. ed. (Hanover, N.H.: University Press of New England, 1981), p. 7.

18. Cf. the excellent discussion in Barbara Adam, *Time and Social Theory* (Philadelphia: Temple University Press, 1990), pp. 112–13.

19. Edward Thompson, "Time, Work-Discipline, and Industrial Capitalism," *Past and Present* 36 (1967), p. 61.

20. Stephen Meyer, *The Five Dollar Day: Labor Management and Social Control in the Ford Motor Company 1908–1921* (Albany: State University of New York Press, 1981), p. 12.

21. Quoted in David Montgomery, *Worker's Control in America: Studies in the History of Work Technology and Labor Struggles* (Cambridge, U.K.: Cambridge University Press, 1979), p. 118.

22. Frederick W. Taylor, *The Principles of Scientific Management* (New York: W. W. Norton, 1967).

23. David F. Nobel, *Forces of Production: A Social History of Industrial Automation* (New York: Alfred A. Knopf, 1984), p. 37.

24. Daniel Bell, "Work and Its Discontents," in Bell, *The End of Ideology*, repr. (Cambridge, Mass: Harvard University Press, 1988), p. 230.

25. Max Weber, *Economy and Society*, Vol. 2, ed. Guenther Roth and Claus Wittich (Berkeley: University of California Press, 1978), p. 1156.

26. Bell, p. 235.

27. Ibid., p. 233.

28. Cf. Anthony Giddens, *The Constitution of Society: Outline of a Theory of Structuration* (Cambridge, U.K.: Polity Press, 1984).

29. John Locke, *Essay Concerning Human Understanding*, ed. A. C. Fraser (New York: Dover, 1959), 1:458–59; David Hume, *A Treatise of Human Nature*, in *The Philosophy of David Hume*, ed. V. C. Chappell (New York: Modern Library, 1963), p. 176.

30. Cf. Edmund Leach, "Two Essays Concerning the Symbolic Representation of Time," in Leach, *Rethinking Anthropology* (London: Athlone, 1968), pp. 124–36.

31. Michael Hammer and James Champy, *Re-engineering the Corporation* (New York: Harper Business, 1993), p. 48.

32. Eric K. Clemons, "Using Scenario Analysis to Manage the Strategic Risks of Reengineering," *Sloan Management Review*, 36:4 (Summer 1995), p. 62.

33. Cf. Scott Lash and John Urry, *The End of Organized Capitalism* (Madison: University of Wisconsin Press, 1987), pp. 196–231.

34. Both results reported in Eileen Applebaum and Rosemary Batt, *The New American Workplace* (Ithaca N.Y.: Cornell University Press, 1993), p. 23.

35. Bennett Harrison, *Lean and Mean* (New York: Basic Books, 1994) pp. 72–73.

36. Michael J. Piore and Charles F. Sabel, *The Second Industrial Divide: Possibilities for Prosperity* (New York: Basic Books, 1984) p. 17.

37. Deborah Morales, *Flexible Production: Restructuring of the International Automobile Industry* (Cambridge, U.K.: Polity Press, 1994), p. 6.

38. Cf. Michel Albert, *Capitalism Against Capitalism*, translated by Paul Haviland (London: Whurr, 1993).

39. Rood Lubbers, "Globalization and the Third Way," paper presented to the Bertelsmann Foundation Forum on Democracy, Oct. 1997.

40. Simon Head, "The New, Ruthless Economy," *New York Review of Books*, Feb. 29, 1996, p. 47. I am much indebted to this excellent essay for its clear account of income inequality.

41. Paul Krugman "The Right, The Rich, and the Facts," *American Prospect* 11 (Fall 1992), pp. 19–31.

42. *Economist*, Nov. 5, 1994, p. 19.

43. Alan Greenspan, quoted in *Wall Street Journal*, July 20, 1995; Robert Reich, "The Revolt of the Anxious Class," a speech given to the Democratic Leadership Council, Nov. 22, 1994, p. 3.

44. Cf. "Making Companies Efficient," *Economist*, Dec. 21, 1996, p. 97.

45. Harrison, p. 47.

46. Data on employment from Manuel Castells, *The Network Society*, Vol. 1 (Oxford, U.K.: Blackwell, 1997), pp. 162–63. Data on gender and income from David Card, "Trends in the Level of Inequality of Wages and Incomes in the United States," paper presented at Council on Work conference, 1997.

47. Cf. Lotte Bailyn, *Breaking the Mold: Men, Women, and Time in the New Workplace* (New York: Free Press, 1993).

48. Cf. Genevieve Capowski, "The Joy of Flex," *Management Review*

(American Management Association), March 1996, pp. 12–18.

49. Jeremy Rifkin, *The End of Work* (New York: Putnam, 1995).

50. Katherine Newman, "School, Skill, and Human Capital in the Low Wage World," paper to be presented at Council on Work conference, forthcoming.

51. Stanley Aronowitz and William DiFazio, *The Jobless Future* (Minneapolis: University of Minnesota Press, 1994), p. 110.

52. Sherry Turkle, *Life on the Screen* (New York: Simon & Schuster, 1995), first sentence p. 64, second sentence note 20, p. 281.

53. Quoted in Sherry Turkle, "Seeing Through Computers," *American Prospect*, 31 (March–April 1997), p. 81.

54. Ibid., p. 82.

55. Ulrich Beck, *Risk Society*, translated by Mark Ritter (London: Sage, 1992), p. 19.

56. Cf. Robert Johansen and Rob Swigart, *Upsizing the Individual in the Downsized Organization* (Reading, Mass.: Addison-Wesley, 1994), p. 137.

57. Richard Sennett, *The Fall of Public Man* (New York: Knopf, 1977), p. 81.

58. Quoted in Peter Bernstein, *Against the Gods: The Remarkable Story of Risk* (New York: Wiley, 1996), p. 119.

59. John Maynard Keynes, *A Treatise on Probability* (London: Macmillan, 1921), pp. 3–4.

60. Amos Tversky, "The Psychology of Risk," in William Sharpe, ed., *Quantifying the Market Risk Premium Phenomenon for Investment Decision Making* (Charlottesville: Institute of Chartered Financial Analysts, 1990), p. 75.

61. Cf. Daniel Kahneman and Amos Tversky, "Prospect Theory: An Analysis of Decision under Risk," *Econometrica* 47:2 (1979), pp. 263–91.

62. Bernstein, p. 272.

63. Cf. Ronald Burt, *Structural Holes: The Social Structure of Competition* (Cambridge, Mass.: Harvard University Press, 1992); and, by contrast, James Coleman, "Social Capital in the Creation of Human Capital," *American Journal of Sociology* 94 (1988), pp. S95–S120.

64. Manuel Castells, *The Network Society*, 1 (Oxford: Blackwell, 1996), pp. 219–20.

65. Cf. Lash and Urry.

66. Cf. Rosabeth Moss Kantor, *When Giants Dance* (New York: Simon & Schuster, 1989).

67. Bureau of Labor Statistics, *Monthly Labor Review* 115:7 (July 1992), p. 7.

68. Krugman quoted in *New York Times*, Feb. 16, 1997, [national edition], section 3, p. 10.

69. Felix Rohatyn, "Requiem for a Democrat," speech delivered at Wake Forest University, March 17, 1995.

70. Cf. Michael Young, *Meritocracy* (London: Penguin, 1971).

71. Cf. Robert Frank and Philip Cook, *The Winner-Take-All Society* (New York: Free Press, 1995).

72. Ibid., p. 101.

73. Smith, pp. 107, 109.

74. Cf. Gregory Bateson, *Steps to an Ecology of Mind* (San Francisco: Chandler, 1972); Leon Festinger, *Conflict, Decision and Dissonance* (Stanford, Calif.: Stanford University Press, 1967); Richard Sennett, The Uses of Disorder (New York: Knopf, 1970).

75. Cf. Anne Marie Guillemard, "Travailleurs vieillissants et marché du travail en Europe," in *Travail et emploi*, Sept. 1993, pp. 60–79. My thanks to Manuel Castells for the graph containing these numbers.

76. Castells, p. 443.

77. Katherine Newman, *Falling from Grace* (New York: Free Press, 1988), p. 70.

78. Ibid., p. 65.

79. Cf. Albert Hirschmann, *Exit, Voice, Loyalty* (Cambridge, Mass.: Harvard University Press, 1970).

80. Cf. Jon Clarke, Ian McLoughlin, Howard Rose, and Robin King, *The Process of Technological Change* (Cambridge, U.K.: Cambridge University Press, 1988).

81. *The Downsizing of America* (New York: Times Books, 1996), pp. 7–8.

82. Oscar Wilde, *The Picture of Dorian Gray* (London: Penguin, 1984), p. 6.

83. Hesiod, *Works and Days*, translated by A. N. Athanassakis (Baltimore: Johns Hopkins, 1983), lines 410–13.

84. Hesiod, *Works and Days*, lines 176–78, quoted in M. I. Finley, *The Ancient Economy*, 2nd ed. (London: Hogarth Press, 1985), p. 81.

85. Virgil *Georgics*, 1.318ff., my translation.

86. Ibid. 2.497ff.

87. Pico della Mirandola, *Oration on the Dignity of Man*, translated by Charles Glenn Wallis (New York: Bobbs-Merrill, 1965), p. 6.

88. Ibid., p. 5.

89. Ibid., p. 24.

90. St. Augustine and Bishop Tyndale quoted in Stephen Greenblatt, *Renaissance Self-Fashioning* (Chicago: University of Chicago Press, 1980), p. 2.

91. My reading of Luther is based on the superb commentary of Jaroslav Pelikan, *Reformation of Church and Dogma*, vol. 4 of *The Christian Tradition* (Chicago: University of Chicago Press, 1984), esp. pp. 127–67.

92. Ibid., p. 131.

93. Cf. Michel Foucault, *Discipline and Punish*, translated by Alan Sheridan (New York: Pantheon, 1977).

94. United States Department of Labor, *What Work Requires of Schools: A SCANS Report for America 2000* (Washington, D.C.: 1991).

95. Charles N. Darrah, *Learning and Work: An Exploration in Industrial Ethnography* (New York: Garland Publishing, 1996), p. 27.

96. Ibid.

97. Laurie Graham, *On the Line at Subaru-Isuzu* (Ithaca, N.Y.: Cornell University Press, 1995), p. 108.

98. Ibid., pp.106ff.

99. Gideon Kunda, *Engineering Culture: Control and Commitment in a High-Tech Corporation* (Philadelphia: Temple University Press, 1992), p. 156.

100. Darrah, p. 167.

101. Graham, p. 116.

102. Eileen Applebaum and Rosemary Batt, *The New American Workplace* (Ithaca, N.Y.: Cornell University Press, 1994), p. 22.

103. Hammer and Champy, p. 65.

104. Quoted in *New York Times*, Feb. 13, 1996, pp. D1, D6.

105. Harley Shaikin, *Work Transformed: Automation and Labor in the Computer Age* (New York: Henry Holt, 1985), p. 82.

106. Richard Rorty, *Contingency, Irony, and Solidarity* (Cambridge, U.K.: Cambridge University Press, 1989), pp. 73–74.

107. Ibid.

108. Ibid., p. 91.

109. Walter Lippmann, *Drift and Mastery* (New York: Mitchell Kennerly, 1914), p. xvi.

110. Ibid., pp. 196, 211.

111. Cf. Henry James, *The American Scene* (Bloomington, Ind.: Indiana University Press, 1968).

112. Cf. Edward Thompson, *The Making of the English Working*

Class (New York: Vintage, 1978).

113. Olivier Zunz, *Making America Corporate* (New York: Oxford University Press, 1990).

114. Lippmann, p. 267.

115. Ibid., p. 269.

116. The best general history of IBM is, to date, Paul Carroll, *Big Blues: The Unmaking of IBM* (New York: Crown Paperbacks, 1993).

117. Richard Thomas DeLamarter, *Big Blue: IBM's Use and Abuse of Power* (New York: Dodd, Mead, 1986), p. 3.

118. William Rodgers, *Think: A Biography of the Watsons and IBM* (New York: Stein and Day, 1969), p. 100.

119. William Sampson, *Company Man* (New York: Random House, 1995), p. 224.

120. Ibid., p. 256.

121. Quoted in *New York Times*, Feb. 13, 1996, pp. D1, D6.

122. Michel Foucault, *Résumé des cours*, 1970–1982 (Paris: Julliard, 1989), p. 123, my translation.

123. Jean-Jacques Rousseau, *The Confessions*, translated by J. H. Cohen (New York: Penguin, 1954), p. 26.

124. Ibid., p. 126.

125. Johann Wolfgang von Goethe, *Poetry and Truth*, translated by R.O. Moon (Washington, D.C.: Public Affairs Press, 1949), p. 692.

126. Katherine Newman, *Falling from Grace: The Experience of Downward Mobility in the American Middle Class* (New York: Free Press, 1988), pp. 93–94.

127. Friedreich Nietzsche, *Thus Spoke Zarathustra*, translated by R. J. Hollingdale (London: Penguin, 1969), p. 163.

128. Salman Rushdie, *Imaginary Homelands* (London: Granta Books, 1991), p. 12.

129. Cf. Zygmunt Bauman, *Postmodern Ethics* (Oxford: Blackwell, 1993); Mark Taylor, *Disfiguring* (Chicago: University of Chicago Press, 1993).

130. William Mitchell, *City of Bits* (Cambridge, Mass.: MIT Press, 1995), p. 28.

131. Turkle, *Life on the Screen*, p. 13.

132. Fredric Jameson, *Post-Modernism, or the Cultural Logic of Late Capitalism* (Chapel Hill: Duke University Press), p. 90.

133. Cf. Saskia Sassen, *The Global City* (Princeton, N.J.: Princeton University Press, 1990).

134. John Bowlby, *Separation* (New York: Basic Books, 1973), p. 359.

135. Cf. Louis Dumont, *Homo Hierarchicus: The Caste System and*

Its Implications, translated by Mark Sainsbury et al. (Chicago: University of Chicago Press, 1980); Takeo Doi, *The Anatomy of Dependence*, translated by John Bester (New York: Kodansha, 1973).

136. Jacques Savary, *Le parfait négotiant* (Paris, 1675; 1713), p. 1.

137. Robert de Montesquieu, *Esprit des Lois*, XX, i.

138. Cf. Lewis Coser, *The Functions of Social Conflict* (New York: Free Press, 1976).

139. Cf. Amy Gutmann and Dennis Thompson, *Democracy and Disagreement* (Cambridge, Mass.: Harvard University Press, 1996).

140. These distinctions, as made by Jean Martineau, are based on Heidegger's concept of *Selb-Standigkeit*, as in Heidegger, *Being and Time*, translated by John MacQuarrie et al. (New York: Harper, 1967), p. 351.

141. Emmanuel Levinas, *Otherwise Than Being*, translated by A. Lingis (The Hague: M. Nijhoff, 1974), pp. 180ff.

142. Paul Ricoeur, *Oneself as Another*, translated by K. Blamey (Chicago: University of Chicago Press, 1992), pp. 165–68.

143. Hans-Georg Gadamer, *Philosophical Hermeneutics*, translated by David Linge (Berkeley: University of California Press, 1976), p. 55; Hans-Georg Gadamer, *Truth and Method*, translated by Garrett Barden and John Cumming (New York: Seabury Press, 1975), p. 245.

Index

accountants, 19–20
achievement, cumulative, 15–16, 30, 43
acting, 34, 37
advertising agencies, 77–80, 83, 84, 88, 91–97, 98, 106–9, 142
agriculture, 99–101, 102
Åkerström, Malin, 115
Albert, Michel, 53
alcoholics, 107
alienation, 70
ambiguously lateral moves, 85, 88
ambition, 18, 78–80
American Dream, 15, 20
American Management Association (AMA), 50
Anglo-American model, 53–55, 139
Anglo-Saxon Protestants, 65
anxiety, 9, 28, 79, 90–91, 97
Appelbaum, Eileen, 113
Applebaum, Herbert, 33
archipelago organization, 23, 55
architects, 73
Aronowitz, Stanley, 73
assembly line, 51–52, 113
Ate, 81
ATT, 22, 114, 125, 146
Augustine, St., 101, 102
authority, 21, 25–26, 28, 84, 96, 108–9, 114–16
automobile industry, 39–43, 51–52, 96, 98–99, 112, 113, 115, 117

Bailyn, Lotte, 58
bakeries, 33, 64–75, 86–87, 88, 98–99, 117, 137, 141, 146
Balzac, Honoré de, 80
Bateson, Gregory, 91
Batt, Rosemary, 113
Bauman, Zygmunt, 133
Beck, Ulrich, 80
Bell, Daniel, 41, 43, 52, 59, 86
bells, church, 36, 101
Benedictines, 36
Bernoulli, Daniel, 81
Bernoulli, Jacob, 81, 82
Bernstein, Peter, 83
Beruf, 121
betrayal, 115, 124–26, 128, 131
Bill for Establishing Religious Freedom (Jefferson), 38
blacks, 17, 27, 65, 67, 69, 70
Blum, Leon, 121
bosses, 111, 112, 113, 114, 115, 117, 126
Bowlby, John, 140
brand names, 56
Bunnell, Sterling, 40
Bunyan, John, 134–35
bureaucracy:
    decentralized, 19–20, 23, 48–49, 55, 57
    disciplined, 41
    flexibility vs., 9–10, 47, 50, 56–57, 121–26, 141
    government, 53–55

bureaucracy (*continued*)
  hierarchy of, 41, 42, 123
  risk and, 84, 89–90, 139
  stability and, 16, 23, 31, 66
  stagnation and, 18, 32, 45, 47, 50, 96
Burt, Ronald, 84, 85
business cycle, 22, 56
businesses, small, 78
"buzz," 78, 79, 107

California Management Review, 93
Calvin, John, 104, 109
Candide (Voltaire), 35
capital:
  "impatient," 22–23
  social, 85
  supply of, 129
capitalism:
  aesthete's distaste for, 119–20
  community and, 136–39, 146–48
  flexible, 9–10, 85, 117, 120, 121–22, 146–48
  industrial, 32, 39, 43, 50, 119, 121, 140, 146
  paternal, 122–23, 125, 133
  state, 54
  work ethic and, 103, 105–6
capitalists, 61–62, 63
careers:
  definition of, 9, 120, 147
  failure and, 119–22
  length of, 92–93
  relocation and, 18–21, 22, 29, 86–88, 156
  see also jobs
Carroll, Paul, 125
Castells, Manuel, 85, 93
Catholicism, 103, 104
Champy, James, 22, 49, 114
change:
  consequences of, 30–31
  flexibility and, 47–48, 49, 50–51, 52, 108, 114
  irreversible, 49, 117
  narrative and, 131–32
  openness to, 18, 108
  personal needs and, 147–48
  technological, 94–97

chaos, 81–82, 84–85, 99, 101, 102–3
character:
  class and, 64–65, 71
  community and, 130, 133–34, 135, 136–48
  corrosion of, 30–31, 37–38, 84, 146–47
  definition of, 10
  ethical nature of, 10, 29, 20
  personal history and, 38, 121
  personality vs., 10
  risk and, 80–81, 84, 90, 117
  self-constancy of, 145–46
  work ethic and, 98–100, 103, 116–17
children:
  labor by, 33–34, 35, 93
  relocation and, 29
  values learned by, 21, 25–26, 28, 30–31
Christianity, 101–6, 130
church bells, 36, 101
City of Bits (Mitchell), 133–34
class:
  character and, 64–65, 71
  consciousness of, 64–67, 71, 74
  definition of, 64–65, 71
  divisions of, 74
  ethnicity and, 65, 66, 67, 71, 75
  labor and, 65–66
  Marxist view of, 65, 69
  race and, 17, 27, 65, 67, 69, 71
  status and, 17, 64, 67, 120
  see also middle class; working class
Clemons, Erik, 49
clerical workers, 19–20
clocks, 36
Cobb, Jonathan, 10, 11, 15, 65
cognitive dissonance, 90–91, 144
Coleman, James, 85
commitment, 10, 24, 25, 26, 30, 31, 62, 70–71, 138, 142, 143, 147
communication:
  conflict and, 94, 143–45
  responsibility and, 114–15
  specialized information and, 107
Communion, 48

Communism, 111
communitarianism, 142–43
communities:
  capitalism and, 136–39, 146–48
  character and, 130, 133–34, 135,
    136–48
  local, 20–21, 130, 135
competition, 105, 111, 118, 123
computer-assisted design (CAD), 73, 74
computers:
  breakdown of, 72–73
  industry for, 23–24, 122–35, 136,
    138, 141–42, 145, 147
  jobs influenced by, 19–20, 44, 52,
    67–68, 70, 71–73, 74, 155
  mainframe, 129
  personal, 56, 123, 129
Confessions (Rousseau), 131
Confessions (St. Augustine), 101
conformity, 108
conservatism, 27–28
constance à soi, 145
consulting firms, 19, 21, 25, 49, 95–96,
    124, 139
consumerism, 22, 51, 64, 75, 105
contracts, 19, 22, 79, 107–8, 124
control, 19–20, 27, 28–30, 31, 37,
    53–55, 58–59
Cook, Philip, 89, 90
cooperation, 99, 112, 115
corporations:
  culture of, 91, 126, 129, 137,
    141–42
  merger of, 48
  organization of, 22, 23
  public offerings of, 24
  reinvention of, 49–50, 51, 55
Coser, Lewis, 143
crafts, 65–66
creative destruction, 30, 43, 80
culture shock, 78–80
cyberspace, 133–34

Darrah, Charles, 111, 112
data entry, 23–24, 44
Davos, Switzerland, 60–63, 75, 80, 85,
    117, 147–48
"deadwood," 95
de Beauvoir, Simone, 64

decision-making, 28–29, 52, 85, 94,
    122–23
Defert, Daniel, 33
delayering, 48–49, 55
democracy, 64
depression, 83, 117
deskilling, 95
Diderot, Denis, 32–35, 36, 37, 44–45,
    48, 144
DiFazio, William, 73
disorientation, 85–88
Doi, Takeo, 140
Dole, Elizabeth, 110
domus, 33
Dostoevsky, Fyodor, 83
downsizing, 19, 29–30, 49, 50, 86, 114,
    118, 123–27, 146
downward mobility, 132
Drift and Mastery (Lippmann),
    119–22
"driven man," 105–6, 109, 116, 119
Dumont, Louis, 140

Economist, 54
economy:
  domus, 33
  flexibility of, 10, 52, 110
  global, 22, 56, 126, 127, 128, 129,
    136–37
  models of, 53–55
education, 15, 17, 32, 53, 88–89, 116,
    156
e-mail, 20, 59
employees:
  accountability of, 113, 114–16,
    120–27, 130
  blue-collar, 15–18, 50, 114–15
  experience of, 91–97, 98, 110
  full-time, 57, 58
  loyalty of, 10, 24–25, 26, 30, 96,
    122–23, 125, 145
  middle-aged, 49, 77, 79–80, 91–97,
    122, 124, 134, 144, 146, 153
  morale of, 50, 125–26
  nonunion, 69–70
  part-time, 57–58, 67, 153
  relocation of, 18–21, 86–87
  self-awareness of, 46–47, 70–71,
    74–75, 145–46, 147

employees (*continued*)
　surveillance of, 20, 58–59
　temporary, 22
　white-collar, 50, 114–15, 155
employment, 54, 55, 149, 150
Encyclopedia (Diderot), 32–35, 144
"engineering rationality," 41
engineers, 73, 94–96, 134
Enrico (fictitious name), 15–18, 19,
　　　21, 22, 26, 27, 29, 30, 43,
　　　44, 66, 98, 117, 146
entrepreneurs, 30, 31, 43, 47, 80, 119,
　　　147
*Essay Concerning Human Under-
　　　standing* (Locke), 46
ethnicity, 65, 66, 67, 71, 75, 98–99
Everts, Rodney (fictitious name),
　　　69–70, 71, 87, 137

factories:
　automobile, 39–43, 51–52, 96,
　　　98–99, 112, 113, 115, 117
　paper, 33–35, 36, 45, 65, 144
　pin, 36–39, 40, 43, 44, 55, 57, 58,
　　　59, 65, 75
failure, 118–35
　careers and, 119–22
　consequences of, 78–79, 80, 107–9
　drift and, 119, 122, 132–34
　fear of, 125–26, 127, 134, 138
　middle class and, 118, 120, 132
　narratives of, 118, 119, 120, 122,
　　　129, 131–35, 141, 145, 147
　responsibility for, 128–35
　risk and, 76–80, 90–91, 129, 130,
　　　133
　success vs., 118–19
　taboos of, 118, 132
　victimization and, 118, 124–26,
　　　128, 131, 132, 133
family:
　authority in, 21, 25–26, 28
　flexibility and, 25–26
　jobs and, 15, 21, 25–27, 29, 30, 33,
　　　36, 57–59, 66
　myths of, 17
　values of, 138–39, 143
fast-food restaurants, 64, 72
fear, 82, 125–26, 127, 134, 138

Festinger, Lionel, 91
Fibonacci, Leonardo, 81–82
Fichte, Johann Gottlieb, 17
Flavia (fictitious name), 15, 19, 57
flexibility, 46–63
　age and, 91–97
　bureaucracy vs., 9–10, 47, 50,
　　　56–57, 121–26, 141
　capitalism and, 9–10, 85, 117, 120,
　　　121–22, 146–48
　change and, 47–48, 49, 50–51, 52,
　　　108, 114
　commitment and, 62, 70–71, 147
　control and, 28–30, 31, 58–59
　definition of, 46
　of economy, 10, 52, 110
　elements of, 47–57, 137
　families and, 25–26
　fragmentation and, 62–63
　in management, 19–20, 23, 32, 37,
　　　55, 56, 86–87, 110–17
　personal freedom and, 47, 58–59,
　　　60, 62–63
　political aspect of, 52–55
　in production, 47, 51–55, 59, 87,
　　　123, 137
　risk and, 45, 62–63, 75, 80–81,
　　　89–97
　routine vs., 44–45, 47, 59
　self-awareness and, 46–47, 70–71,
　　　74–75
　skill vs., 72–73, 74
　specialization and, 51, 67
　teamwork and, 106, 108, 116–17
　technology and, 52, 67
flextime, 57–59, 67, 70
focal attention, 90–91, 144
Ford, Henry, 39
Fordism, 39, 44, 51, 59
Ford Motor Company, 39–40, 43, 96
Fortuna, 81
Foucault, Michel, 106, 130–31
"Foundations of Natural Law"
　　　(Fichte), 17
France, 92
Frank, Robert, 89, 90
Franklin, Benjamin, 105
freedom, personal, 47, 58–59, 60,
　　　62–63

free enterprise, 9, 35, 36, 53
Functions of Social Conflict, The
    (Coser), 143

Gadamer, Hans-Georg, 147
Gambler, The (Dostoevsky), 83
gambling, 82–84
Gates, Bill, 61, 62, 70
General Electric, 41
General Motors, 41–43, 86
Georgics (Virgil), 100–101
German-Americans, 40
Germany, 92–93
Gerstner, Louis, 123, 127, 128
Giddens, Anthony, 44–45, 48, 144
goals:
    long-term, 10, 22
    short-term, 10, 22–27
Goethe, Johann Wolfgang von, 131–32
government:
    bureaucracy of, 53–55
    control by, 27, 53–55, 119
Graham, Laurie, 112, 113, 115, 144
Granovetter, Mark, 24
Great Britain, 53, 54, 92, 96
Great Depression, 16, 31
Greek-Americans, 65–66, 69, 71, 75,
    98–99, 117
gross domestic product (GDP), 50
guilt, 29–30, 118, 140, 141
Gutmann, Amy, 144

Hammer, Michael, 49, 114
Harrison, Bennett, 22, 56
Hawthorn plant, 41
Head, Simon, 54
health care, 53
Hesiod, 99–101, 102, 119
Hidden Injuries of Class, The
    (Sennett and Cobb), 10, 11,
    15, 64
hierarchy, logic of, 41, 42
Highland Park factory, 39–40, 43, 96
Hirschmann, Albert, 94, 140, 144
Hoccleve, Thomas, 31
holes, structural, 84–85, 87
"hollowing," 56
homo faber, 101–2, 106
Horace, 10, 146

Hume, David, 46

IBM, 25, 122–35, 136, 138, 141–42,
    145, 147
immigrants, 16, 65, 119–20, 121, 127
India, 126, 128, 129, 138
individualism, 64, 105, 109, 113, 121,
    140, 142–43
information:
    sharing of, 111
    specialized, 107
initial public offerings, 24
Institutes (Calvin), 104
institutions, social, 47–51, 59, 87, 99,
    121, 133, 137
Internet, 61, 129
investments, financial, 81
Irish-Americans, 17
"iron cage," 16
irony, 116
Israel, 53
Italian-Americans, 65, 66, 67
Italy, 51, 53

James, Henry, 120
Jameson, Fredric, 134
janitors, 15–16, 21, 26
Japan, 52, 53, 54, 57, 113
Jason (fictitious name), 124, 126
Jeannette (fictitious name), 18–20,
    23–24, 29, 57, 59
Jefferson, Thomas, 38
Jesus Christ, 102
Jim (fictitious name), 128, 129
jobs:
    categories of, 85, 86
    change of, 18–19, 22, 86–88, 156
    computerization and, 19–20, 44,
        52, 67–68, 70, 71–73, 74,
        155
    definition of, 9, 120
    families and, 15, 21, 25–27, 29, 30,
        33, 36, 57–59, 66
    market for, 54, 55, 87, 88–89, 97
    see also employees

Kahneman, Daniel, 82, 83
Kantor, Rosabeth Moss, 86
Keynes, John Maynard, 82

Kim (fictitious name), 129
Kotter, John, 25, 139
Krugman, Paul, 54, 89, 127
Kunda, Gideon, 112

labor:
  attachment and, 70–71
  cheap, 33–34, 70, 72, 87, 93, 95,
    126
  child, 33–34, 35, 93
  class and, 65–66
  compressed schedules of, 58
  demeaning, 45, 67–71, 98, 106
  Diderot's views on, 32–35, 36, 37,
    44–45, 48, 144
  dignity of, 33
  division of, 35–39, 40, 55
  efficiency of, 40–41, 49, 50
  engagement with, 64–75, 110, 117,
    137, 145
  female, 15, 18–19, 57–58, 71, 153
  foreign, 126–28, 129, 131, 133, 138
  at home, 33, 36, 57–59
  legibility of, 68
  location of, 58–59, 133–34, 136–38
  long-term, 20–21, 24–25, 143
  management vs., 41, 48–49, 50, 55,
    56, 86–87, 111–17, 123
  manual, 120
  Marxist view of, 39, 44
  mechanization of, 40, 67, 68,
    71–73, 98, 141
  replacement, 49
  rhythm of, 34, 35, 39, 48
  routine in, 32–45, 47, 59, 103, 144
  short-term, 25, 27, 84, 106, 110,
    111, 124
  skilled, 39–40, 65–66, 69, 72–73,
    74, 89, 95–97, 99, 110, 120,
    128
  Smith's views on, 32, 35–39, 40,
    41, 43, 44, 45, 47, 55, 59,
    73, 75, 90, 144
  specialized, 40, 51, 67
  standards for, 128, 129, 137,
    145–46
  supply of, 88–89, 126, 127, 128,
    129, 138, 146
  unskilled, 71–75, 89

  see also jobs
labor unions, 16, 20, 23, 42–43, 52, 66,
    67, 86, 113, 117, 147, 152,
    157
L'Anglée paper factory, 33–35, 45, 144
Lash, Scott, 50
Leach, Edmund, 47–48
leadership, 90, 108–9, 111, 112, 113,
    115–16, 117
Lean and Mean (Harrison), 56
Leidner, Robin, 112
Levinas, Emmanuel, 145
Liber Abaci (Fibonacci), 81
Lippmann, Walter, 119–22, 129, 131,
    133, 135
listening, 99, 110, 143
Little Lenin Library, 61–62
Lloyd's, 81
Locke, John, 46
loyalty, 10, 24–25, 26, 30, 96, 122–23,
    125, 145
Lubbers, Ruud, 54
luck, 83–84
Luther, Martin, 103–4, 109

McDonald's restaurants, 72
machines, 40, 67, 68, 71–73, 98, 141
Madison, James, 38
Mafia, 65, 66
Magic Mountain, The (Mann), 60
maintien de soi, 145
"mall rats," 21, 28
management:
  challenges to, 94, 144–45
  change of, 69
  as "coaches," 115–16
  flexible, 19–20, 32, 37, 55, 56,
    86–87, 110–17
  labor vs., 41, 48–49, 50, 55, 56,
    86–87, 111–17, 123
  software for, 48, 55
  teamwork and, 110–17
Mann, Thomas, 60
markets:
  consumer-driven, 22
  free, 9, 35, 36, 53
  global, 22, 56
  growth of, 38
  job, 54, 55, 87, 88–89, 97

niches in, 51
responsiveness to, 45, 67
unpredictability of, 47, 51
winner-take-all, 89–90, 118, 146
Marx, Karl, 39, 44, 70
Marxism, 39, 44, 65, 69, 119, 146
Massachusetts Institute of
    Technology, 73
mastery, 110–22, 130–31
Mayo, Elton, 41
mediation, 108, 109, 117
Meritocracy (Young), 89
metric time, 41, 42–43, 59
Meyer, Stephen, 40
Microsoft, 61, 123
middle class:
    definition of, 64, 71
    failure and, 118, 120, 132
    status and, 120
    values of, 16–17
    women in, 57–58
midlife crisis, 77
Mill, John Stuart, 47, 90
"mill girls," 93
Mitchell, William, 133–34
Montesquieu, 140
Morales, Deborah, 52
mortgages, 43
mutual dependence, 139–42

narratives, 16, 24, 30, 43, 44, 83–84,
    104, 117
    of failure, 118, 119, 120, 122, 129,
        131–35, 141, 145, 147
nature, 99–100, 109
neoliberalism, 54
Netherlands, 54
networking, 19, 20, 77–89, 107, 108
network organization, 23, 48, 56,
    84–85, 136, 137, 146
neutrality, 115
Newman, Katherine, 72, 93, 132
New York Times, 97
Nietzsche, Friedrich, 132
Noble, David, 41
"no long term," 22, 24, 25, 31

Oration on the Dignity of Man (Pico
    della Mirandola), 101–2

orphanages, 27, 28

paper factories, 33–35, 36, 45, 65, 144
Paradox of Acting (Diderot), 34
parasites, social, 18, 27, 139–40, 142
parfait négotiant, Le (Savary), 140
Paul (fictitious name), 124, 126, 130
peer pressure, 113, 114
pensions, 16, 53, 66
physicians, 127
Pico della Mirandola, Giovanni, 101–2,
    104, 109, 116–17, 119, 121
Picture of Dorian Grey, The
    (Wilde), 98
Pilgrim's Progress (Bunyan), 134–35
pin factories, 36–39, 40, 43, 44, 55, 57,
    58, 59, 65, 75
Piore, Michael, 51, 67
"pit boys," 93
Powell, Walter, 23
power:
    concentration of, 47, 55–57, 59,
        137
    submission to, 59
    teamwork and, 109, 111, 112–16
predestination, 104–5
prejudice, social, 91–97, 139–40
priests, 48
Principles of Political Economy
    (Mill), 47
probability, 81–82
problem-solving, 91
production:
    computerized, 52
    flexible, 47, 51–55, 59, 87, 123, 137
    teamwork and, 113
productivity, 41, 45, 50, 113, 151
products:
    brand-name, 56
    consumer-friendly, 75
    variety of, 51, 123
profit, 39, 45, 49, 50, 113, 123
programmers, computer, 122–35, 136,
    138, 141–42, 145, 147
*Protestant Ethic and the Spirit of
    Capitalism, The* (Weber),
    102–6
Protestantism, 103–6
Providence, 104, 140

punishment, 106
pyramid organization, 23, 48, 52,
        56–57, 84, 85

race, 17, 27, 65, 67, 69, 71
randomness, 81, 83, 87
reengineering, 49, 51, 93–94, 114, 118
Re-engineering the Corporation
        (Hammer and Champy), 49,
        114
Regiment of Princes, The
        (Hoccleve), 31
regression to the mean, 82, 83
Renaissance, 101–2
responsibility, 28–29, 104, 113,
        114–16, 121, 128–35,
        144–45
retirement, 16, 93, 94, 109
retraining, 95
retrospective losses, 85, 88
Rhine model, 53–55, 139
Rico (fictitious name), 15, 17–31, 38,
        62, 84, 94–96, 98, 117, 118,
        134, 138–39, 143
Ricoeur, Paul, 145–46
risk, 76–97
    age and, 80, 91–97
    ambiguity and, 80, 85
    anxiety and, 9, 28, 79, 90–91, 97
    bureaucracy and, 84, 89–90, 139
    calculation of, 81–84
    character and, 80–81, 84, 90, 117
    culture of, 87, 139–40
    definition of, 81–82
    disorientation and, 85–88
    failure and, 76–80, 90–91, 129,
        130, 133
    fear of, 82
    flexibility and, 45, 62–63, 75,
        80–81, 89–97
    narrative of, 83–84
    necessity of, 18, 28
    psychic, 102
    "repotting" image for, 80–81
    reward and, 146
    social productions of, 80
Rockefeller, John D., 61–62
Rohatyn, Felix, 89
Rorty, Richard, 116

Rose (fictitious name), 76–80, 83, 84,
        87, 91–97, 98, 106–9, 117,
        142
rote learning, 32
Rousseau, Jean-Jacques, 131, 132,
        137–38
routine, 32–45, 47, 59, 103, 144
Rushdie, Salman, 133, 143

Sabel, Charles, 51, 67
safety net, 53, 139, 142
Sampson, Anthony, 125, 141
Sanchez, Arturo, 11
Sassen, Saskia, 136
Savary, Jacques, 140
Schumpeter, Joseph, 30, 31, 43, 80
Second Industrial Divide, The
        (Piore and Sabel), 51
Secretary's Committee on Achieving
        Necessary Skills (SCANS),
        110–11
self-employment, 141
seniority, 16, 42, 96, 110, 117
sensations, 46–47
servants, 120
sexuality, 26
Shaiken, Harley, 114–15, 144
sick leave, 42
Silicon Valley, 18, 20, 129, 130
SimCity, 74
SIMS program, 48, 55
size, logic of, 41–42
skills, 39–40, 65–66, 69, 72–73, 74, 89,
        95–97, 99, 110, 120, 128
sloth, 101, 102–3
Smith, Adam, 32, 35–39, 40, 41, 43,
        44, 45, 47, 55, 59, 73, 75,
        90, 144
social contract, 123
socialism, 43
software management, 48, 55
Spanish Civil War, 61
spontaneity, 37–38, 39, 45, 47, 59, 63
statistical tables, 11, 24, 44, 50,
        149–57
status, 17, 64, 67, 120
Stendhal, 80
stockbrokers, 86
stock markets, 22–23, 51

stoicism, 101
Structural Holes (Burt), 84
Subaru-Isuzu plant, 112, 113, 115
suburbia, 16–17, 20–21
success:
    failure vs., 118–19
    measurement of, 78–80
superficiality, 74–75, 98–99, 106, 108,
        109, 114, 117, 138
survival, 112, 125, 126–27
sympathy, 37–38, 39, 45, 47, 59, 144

Tagwerk, 39, 59
Taylor, Frederick W., 40–41
Taylor, Mark, 133
teamwork, 24, 25, 99, 106–17, 138,
        142, 143, 146
    flexibility and, 106, 108, 116–17
    management and, 110–17
    power and, 109, 111, 112–16
    production and, 113
    work ethic and, 106–17
technology:
    change in, 94–97
    flexibility and, 52, 67
    growth of, 22, 50, 62
    knowledge of, 94–95
television, 26
tenure, 28
Theory of Moral Sentiments, The
        (Smith), 37–38, 39
Thompson, Dennis, 144
Thompson, E. P., 39, 120
Thucydides, 100
Thurow, Lester, 127
Thus Spake Zarathustra
        (Nietzsche), 132
time:
    continuity of, 47–48
    ecclesiastical, 36, 101
    flex-, 57–59, 67, 70
    fragmentation of, 22–27, 30,
        62–63, 98, 133–34
    historical, 102
    linear, 15–16, 17, 18, 22, 30
    mechanical, 36
    metric, 41, 42–43, 59
    organization of, 19–20, 22, 36,
        42–43, 44, 59, 101, 102–3,
        104, 106, 154
    routine and, 32, 35
    skills and passage of, 95–97
    space and, 36
time-motion studies, 40–41
Tocqueville, Alexis de, 64
traders, 38, 39, 47, 90, 140
Treatise on Human Nature, A
        (Hume), 46
Treatise on Probability (Keynes), 82
trust, 24, 31, 140, 141–42, 143
Turkle, Sherry, 74, 134
Tversky, Amos, 82, 83
Tyndale, William, 102

unemployment, 54, 55, 150
United Auto Workers, 42–43
United States:
    as classless society, 64–65
    economy of, 53, 54
unpredictable wage outcomes, 85–86,
        88
*Upsizing the Individual in the
        Downsized Corporation*
        (Johansen and Swigart), 80
upward mobility, 16–18, 21, 65, 85
Urry, John, 50
user-friendliness, 71–72, 98

vacations, 42
values:
    common, 137–39, 143, 147
    family, 138–39, 143
    fixed, 28
    loss of, 20–21, 28
    middle-class, 16–17
    social, 10, 27–28
    teaching of, 21, 25–26, 28, 30–31
    working-class, 15–18
venture capital firms, 18
vertical disaggregation, 49, 55
victimization, 114, 115, 118, 124–26,
        128, 131, 132, 133, 146–47
Vietnamese-Americans, 67, 70, 71,
        111
Virgil, 100–101, 102, 116, 119
vodka, 106–8
"voice," 94, 144–45
Voltaire, 35

vulnerability, 130, 142

wages:
  inequality of, 54, 55, 88–89, 150
  low, 33–34, 70, 72, 87, 93, 95, 126
  trend in, 85–86, 88–89, 156
watches, 36
Watson, Thomas, Jr., 123
Watson, Thomas, Sr., 122–23, 131
"we," 137–39, 143, 147
wealth:
  creation of, 80
  transfer of, 89
Wealth of Nations, The (Smith), 32,
    35–39
Webb, Beatrice, 121
Webb, Sidney, 121
Weber, Max, 16, 99, 102–6, 119, 121
Weisskopf, Victor, 73
welfare, 27, 53, 55, 139, 142
Wilde, Oscar, 98
will, assertion of, 29, 38
Willow Run plant, 41–43, 98–99, 117
women:
  in middle class, 57–58
  in work force, 15, 18–19, 57–58,
    71, 153
"Work and Its Discontents" (Bell),
    41–42
work ethic, 98–117
  capitalism and, 103, 105–6
  character and, 98–100, 103,
    116–17

competition and, 105, 111
delayed gratification and, 98–99,
    102, 109, 116
ethnicity and, 65, 66, 67, 71, 75,
    98–99
history of, 99–106
responsibility and, 104, 113,
    114–16
self-discipline in, 98–103, 105–6
self-fashioning in, 101–2, 106,
    116–17
teamwork and, 106–17
time organized by, 101, 102–3,
    104, 106
working class:
  ethnicity and, 65, 66, 67, 71, 75,
    98–99
  race and, 17, 27, 65, 67, 69, 71
  values of, 15–18
Works and Days (Hesiod), 99–100
World Economic Forum, 60–63, 75,
    80, 85, 117, 147–48
"worldly asceticism," 99, 103, 105,
    109, 116
World War II, 16, 31
Wyatt Companies, 50

Young, Michael, 89

Zunz, Olivier, 120